Conducting Research Surveys via E-Mail and the Web

Matthias Schonlau

Ronald D. Fricker, Jr.

Marc N. Elliott

RAND

Approved for public release; distribution unlimited

This study was conducted by RAND as part of its continuing program of self-sponsored research. The research described in this report was supported through the independent research and development provisions of RAND's contracts for the operation of its Department of Defense federally funded research and development centers: Project AIR FORCE (sponsored by the U.S. Air Force), the Arroyo Center (sponsored by the U.S. Army), and the National Defense Research Institute (sponsored by the Office of the Secretary of Defense, the Joint Staff, the unified commands, and the defense agencies). The RAND Statistics Group also provided additional funding for this research.

Library of Congress Cataloging-in-Publication Data

Schonlau, Matthias, 1967–
    Conducting research surveys via E-mail and the Web / Matthias Schonlau,
Ronald D. Fricker, Jr., Marc N. Elliott.
      p. cm.
    "MR-1480."
    Includes bibliographical references.
    ISBN 0-8330-3110-4
    1. Social sciences—Research—Methodology. 2. Social sciences—Data
processing. 3. Social surveys. 4. Surveys. 5. Electronic mail systems. 6. Telephone
surveys. 7. Internet. I. Fricker, Ronald D., 1960– II. Elliott, Marc N., 1966–
III. Title.

HA29 .S366 2002
001.4'33—dc21

                                     2001048925

RAND is a nonprofit institution that helps improve policy and decisionmaking through research and analysis. RAND® is a registered trademark. RAND's publications do not necessarily reflect the opinions or policies of its research sponsors.

Cover design by Barbara Angell Caslon

Published 2002 by RAND
1700 Main Street, P.O. Box 2138, Santa Monica, CA 90407-2138
1200 South Hayes Street, Arlington, VA 22202-5050
201 North Craig Street, Suite 102, Pittsburgh, PA 15213
RAND URL: http://www.rand.org/
To order RAND documents or to obtain additional information,
contact Distribution Services: Telephone: (310) 451-7002;
Fax: (310) 451-6915; Email: order@rand.org

Low-cost personal computers and the explosive growth of the Internet over the past decade have introduced new methods of conducting research surveys. It is now possible to conduct an entire survey solely through the World Wide Web or by e-mail. But, just as issues were raised about phone and mail surveys when they were first introduced, many researchers and practitioners are trying to determine the best way to conduct Internet surveys and questioning just how scientifically valid Internet-based surveys are.

This book provides practical information for researchers who are contemplating using the Internet in their survey activities. The authors examine the reported strengths and limitations of using the Internet to conduct research surveys and offer guidelines on survey design and implementation. This book should be of interest to social science and public policy researchers, although it is certainly applicable to any form of survey research, including that conducted within the Department of Defense and throughout the armed forces. It should also prove useful to principal investigators, survey coordinators, and survey programmers.

This study was conducted by RAND as part of its continuing program of self-sponsored research. Support was provided through the independent research and development provisions of RAND's contracts for the operation of its Department of Defense federally funded research and development centers: Project AIR FORCE (sponsored by the U.S. Air Force), the Arroyo Center (sponsored by the U.S. Army), and the National Defense Research Institute (sponsored by the Office of the Secretary of Defense, the Joint Staff, the unified commands, and the defense agencies). The RAND Statistics Group also provided additional funding for this research.

CONTENTS

FIGURES

TABLES

The Internet is profoundly changing the way we communicate with one another. One of the most recent new uses of the World Wide Web is as a survey platform. Internet-based surveys, although still in their infancy, are becoming increasingly popular because they are believed to be faster, better, cheaper, and easier to conduct than surveys that use more-traditional telephone or postal mail methods. Based on the evidence in the literature and real-life case studies, this report examines the extent to which these claims hold true. Specifically, it analyzes the advantages and disadvantages of using the Internet—both e-mail and the Web—to conduct research surveys.

This report provides practical information on design and implementation for researchers who are thinking about using the Internet in their survey activities or who are planning to conduct an Internet survey. In addition to our review of the literature on Internet surveys, we base our analysis on a number of other sources, including several institutions with experience in conducting surveys on the Internet, individual researchers who have relied on Web surveys in their studies, and our own personal experiences.

This report addresses three main questions that researchers face with regard to Internet surveys:

- When should an Internet-based survey be considered?
- What type of Internet survey is appropriate for a particular study?
- How should an Internet survey be designed and implemented?

WHEN SHOULD AN INTERNET SURVEY BE CONSIDERED?

Internet surveys may be preferable to mail or telephone surveys in the following cases:

- **The survey can be conducted with a convenience sample.** In a convenience sample, the probability with which a respondent is selected into the sample may not be known. Often, respondents "self-select" into the survey. For example, advertising on Web pages, in newsgroups, and in traditional media can be used to attract a large number of survey respondents.

- **The survey is being conducted in an organization that has a list of e-mail addresses for the target population.** The benefits in terms of cost and timeliness are greatest when the target population can be contacted initially by e-mail. The U.S. Air Force, for example, maintains a standardized e-mail address system, as well as detailed information about individuals on their e-mail list. Such plusses make the Web a logical choice for a survey mode.

- **The target population represents a small slice of the total population.** Contacting very small slices of the population via random digit dialing (RDD) phone surveys is very inefficient and therefore costly. Mail surveys in this case would be less costly but equally inefficient. In pre-recruited panels (in which potential survey respondents are recruited in advance for multiple surveys), the information obtained from panel participants allows for targeting subpopulations directly. The advantages in using prerecruited panels may make it more cost-efficient to contract with a commercial Web survey company that can target any subpopulation directly from its panel database.

- **The sample size is moderately large.** Generally, Web surveys have a larger initial start-up cost than mail or phone surveys, but they have a lower marginal cost per survey respondent. Therefore, the Web is not a cost-efficient medium for surveys with a small number of respondents. Quantifying "small" is difficult and estimates vary considerably with the assumptions being made. In one case, we estimated that adding a Web response option to an existing mail survey is cost effective when at least 580 completed questionnaires are obtained over the Web.

- **The survey contains questions of a particularly sensitive nature.** There may be a bias toward socially acceptable answers (as opposed to more-honest answers that may be less socially acceptable) in surveys in which the interviewee has direct contact with an interviewer. To avoid this bias, Web surveys, as well as mail surveys, are an option.

- **The survey contains a large number of important open-ended questions.** Unlike with mail surveys, Web surveys incur no coding or editing costs because responses are received electronically. There is also some evidence that respondents give longer answers to open-ended questions in electronic surveys than open-ended questions in printed surveys.

- **The survey is a multimedia survey or contains interactive elements.** There is no way, other than using the Web, to conduct a survey with interactive elements at a reasonable cost.

WHAT TYPE OF INTERNET SURVEY IS APPROPRIATE FOR A PARTICULAR STUDY?

There are two main types of survey samples: convenience samples and probability samples. (We also discuss also a hybrid approach that combines the two.) *Convenience samples* arise from uncontrolled instrument distribution or self-selection (that is, volunteering) into a survey. Convenience samples are often less costly to generate than probability samples, but statistical inference becomes problematic. Convenience samples are useful to researchers in developing research hypotheses, defining ranges of alternatives, and conducting qualitative data analysis. With certain assumptions, convenience samples can be useful for model-based inference.

Probability samples (also called *random samples*) are samples in which the probability with which an individual was selected into the sample can be determined. Probability samples can be classified into three types: those taken from *closed populations* (such as from organizations that maintain lists of their members in some form), *general populations,* and *pre-recruited panels.* In closed populations, it is often possible to draw a probability sample that allows for contacting potential survey respondents via e-mail. This capability makes a Web survey particularly easy to conduct.

In general populations, an e-mail directory of the population does not exist. Without such a list, it is impossible to determine the selection probabilities; therefore, it is not possible to draw a probability sample from a general population. If a probability sample is desired from a general population, the population must be contacted by mail or by phone. The only possible exception to this is with pre-recruited panels. If an appropriate pre-recruited panel exists for the population of interest, it is possible to send the panel invitations via e-mail to participate in a survey.

We also investigated whether it is possible to combine a convenience sample and a probability sample to achieve better results. The hope was that if the bias of estimates from the convenience sample was not too large, then the combined sample might be more precise than the probability sample. We found that it is not useful to combine the samples unless the bias from the convenience sample is known to be very small and the probability sample has at least several thousand responses. Because the size of the bias is not known in advance and probability samples are often smaller in size, this theory is not useful in practice.

HOW SHOULD AN INTERNET SURVEY BE DESIGNED AND IMPLEMENTED?

Based on our experience with Web surveys, we provide a number of tips on design and implementation, which are briefly listed here and discussed in Chapter Five.

In designing an effective Web survey questionnaire, we recommend the following:

- List only a few questions per screen.

- Eliminate unnecessary questions.

- Use graphics sparingly.

- Be aware of how respondents may interpret questions in light of accompanying graphics.

- Use matrix questions sparingly.

- Reduce response errors by restricting response choices.

- Force answers only on rare occasions.

- Make error or warning messages as specific as possible.

- Always password-protect Web surveys.

- Ensure that respondents' privacy and their perception of privacy are protected.

- Provide some indication of survey progress.

- Allow respondents to interrupt and reenter the survey.

- Carefully handle respondents who fail a screening test.

- Give respondents something in return.

- Take advantage of the media's presentation capabilities.

We also offer the following suggestions on automating the survey instrument:

- Automate skip patterns.

- Automatically validate input, if possible.

- Take advantage of the electronic media's ability to track respondent behavior.

- Take into account the cost of automation.

In implementing and fielding the survey, we suggest the following guidelines:

- Thoroughly test the survey.

- If a large number of respondents are contacted via e-mail, stagger the e-mail invitations.

- Enable respondents to report problems.

- Anticipate potential changes while the survey is in the field.

- Make sure that researchers or survey sponsors can access the Web survey during the fielding.

- Remember to follow up on incomplete surveys.

ARE INTERNET SURVEYS FASTER, BETTER, CHEAPER, OR EASIER TO CONDUCT?

The benefits of Internet-based surveys are often exaggerated. The most commonly heard claim is that Internet surveys are always faster, better, and cheaper than conventional survey methods. Also, because it is relatively easy to create Web sites, it is often assumed that Web surveys are easier for researchers to field and easier for respondents to complete. This report offers important qualifications to these claims.

Are They Faster?

Web surveys are conducted much more quickly than mail or phone surveys when respondents are contacted initially by e-mail. If respondents are initially contacted by mail or phone (instead of by e-mail) for a Web survey, at best only a marginal improvement in overall response times can be expected.

In response to a congressional inquiry, for example, the U.S. Air Force Survey Branch completed an Air Force–wide survey in just 11 days, including design and analysis. The Surveys Branch uses e-mail as the contact mode and the Web as the response mode. In a RAND study of college students and college-bound youth, respondents were contacted by mail and encouraged to respond via the Web. An additional mail response option was sent 35 days after the first mailing. The survey was fielded for a total of 90 days, with a number of mail responses arriving after the 90 days were up.

When a probability sample is required for a general population (such as college-age youth), an e-mail sample frame (an e-mail address directory, for example) is usually not available. However, if a panel of respondents who can serve as the sample frame has already been built, Web surveys can be conducted very quickly indeed. Commercial Web survey companies, such as Knowledge Networks and Harris Interactive, generally field a survey for approximately ten days. Faster turnaround times are possible, but at the expense of a lower response rate.

Are They Better?

The presence of numerous surveys on the Web that are used purely for entertainment purposes can easily cloud one's opinion regarding the quality of Web surveys. With research surveys, the quality of the survey process is at least as important as the number of surveys that are fielded. The number of fielded surveys affects only the statistical error (or variance); the quality of the survey process affects a number of other errors (which collectively might be called "bias").

It is possible with Web surveys to obtain probability samples, which for many research projects are indispensable. When an e-mail sample frame exists, it is fairly easy to obtain a probability sample. When an e-mail sample frame does not exist, obtaining a probability sample for conducting a Web survey is just as difficult as it would be with a mail or phone survey. As far as response rates are concerned, it appears that when only one response option is given, mail response rates are higher than Web or e-mail response rates. When respondents are contacted by postal mail rather than by e-mail, it is desirable to give respondents the option of responding by either the Web or by postal mail to avoid low response rates.

Are They Cheaper?

The general perception that Web surveys are much cheaper to conduct than mail surveys is not necessarily true. There are three main cost components in conducting surveys: mailing, data entry, and labor (design and operations). Cost savings with Web surveys are greatest if respondents can be contacted initially via e-mail. Then there are no mailing or phone costs associated with the invitation to participate in the survey. In addition, Web surveys incur virtually no coding or data-entry costs because the data is captured electronically. Taken together, the savings from these two cost components reduce the per-unit or marginal cost.

Labor costs, however, can be high with Web surveys. The one-time cost for constructing a Web survey is substantial, particularly in cases in which the survey designer has no prior experience with Web surveys. The literature typically neglects labor costs and therefore often concludes that electronic surveys are much cheaper than surveys conducted using more-traditional modes.

Because Web surveys have a higher one-time cost and a lower marginal cost than mail surveys, neither mail surveys nor Web surveys are clearly better than the other in terms of cost. It appears that Web surveys become more economical than mail surveys only when the number of responses reaches a certain threshold—somewhere between a few hundred and a thousand—and in a mixed-mode setting in which the fielding sequence is designed to encourage response via the Internet and avoid incurring costs from using a conventional mode until it is absolutely necessary. However, unanticipated technical problems are likely to arise when a researcher has no prior experience with Web survey programming. Such problems can easily eliminate all potential cost benefits from using the Web.

Are They Easier to Conduct?

Implementing a Web survey is a more technically complicated process than implementing a mail or telephone survey. Survey designers need to specifically address many details related to the technical control of Web surveys (for example, how the respondent will move backward and forward among questions, how to enable input validation, how to use passwords, determining which questions will not be optional), which are either much simpler to address or are not required at all with conventional survey modes. Web surveys also require extensive pretesting to ensure that the questions elicit the desired information and the program works properly across various hardware and software configurations. For survey teams without Web survey experience, these steps often call for more work rather than less.

Our analysis suggests that Web surveys will become more widely used but are unlikely to entirely replace traditional survey modes. Instead, they will become one of a range of survey tools, with their own distinct advantages and disadvantages. For research surveys, the Internet will most likely be used in combination with the telephone or postal mail for best results.

ACKNOWLEDGMENTS

We thank Barbara Sedivi Gaul, Howard Kanarek, and David Mingay of the U.S. Census Bureau for sharing the results of their work at the Computer Assisted Survey Research Office. Charlie Hamilton and Capt. Laura Harding of the U.S. Air Force Surveys Branch of the Air Force Personnel Center provided us with information about the Air Force's survey programs and shared their insights about the use of the Web for conducting surveys. We also acknowledge the kind assistance and comments of Mick Couper at the University of Michigan, which lead to important improvements in this report.

We owe a debt of gratitude to our RAND colleagues who advised and assisted us during this research, including Beth Asch, Tom Bogdon, Chris Corey, Arie Kapteyn, Grant Marshall, Al Robbert, Gery Ryan, and Sandy Berry of the RAND Survey Research Group. Finally, this report was greatly improved with the counsel of our colleagues in the RAND Statistics Group, particularly Sally Morton and Dan McCaffrey, and the efforts of communications analyst Laura Zakaras and the report's editor, Nancy DelFavero.

ACRONYMS

ASCII	American Standard Code for Information Interchange
BBS	Bulletin board system
CAPI	Computer-aided personal interviewing
CASRO	Computer Assisted Survey Research Office (U.S. Census Bureau)
CATI	Computer-aided telephone interviewing
CPS	Current Population Survey
CSAQ	Computerized self-administered questionnaire
DoD	Department of Defense
ESS	Effective sample size
HTML	Hypertext markup language
iid	Independent and identically distributed
MIS	Management information system
MSE	Mean squared error
PIN	Personal Identification Number
RDD	Random digit dialing
TDM	Total (or Tailored) Design Method
TSD	Total Survey Design

URL   Uniform resource locator

USAF   United States Air Force

Chapter One

INTRODUCTION

Before we begin our discussion of the merits, and limitations, of Web and e-mail surveys, it is instructive to note a few things about the survey process in general.

When part of a research program, surveys usually are designed to permit formal statistical inference about some larger population given certain information collected from a subset of that population. Choices in survey design—including those of contact mode, response mode, and sampling methodology—must be made and those choices must be evaluated in light of the cost implications and the subsequent effects those choices may have on data quality and the precision of survey parameter estimates. These choices must be made early in the research planning process and many times are based on what is, and what is not, known from other similar surveys.

The Internet has introduced innovations that have spawned new methods for conducting surveys, most notably surveys done via electronic mail (e-mail) and the World Wide Web.[1] In e-mail surveys, the survey instrument is contained in the main body of the e-mail message or in an e-mail attachment. In many cases, the respondent can complete the survey by simply replying to the original e-mail. Web surveys are "hosted" (that is, they reside) on a Web site. The respondent visits the survey Web site by either clicking a hyperlink in

---

[1]Computer-aided telephone interviewing (CATI) and computer-aided personal interviewing (CAPI) are other notable technological advances in surveying. They are unrelated to the development of the Internet and therefore we do not examine them in this report. In fact, for the purposes of our work, we consider CAPI to be another form of in-person interviewing and CATI to be another form of telephone interviewing.

an e-mail or in another Web site, or by typing the Web address directly into the address box in the browser window.

Internet surveys have been both hyped for their capabilities and criticized for their limitations. To put Web and e-mail surveying in perspective, it is instructive to examine what was written about telephone and mail surveys when they were still regarded as unproven survey methodologies. In 1978, Don Dillman, a noted authority on surveying, said the following about mail and telephone survey questionnaires:

> Neither mail nor telephone has been considered anything more than a poor substitute for the much heralded face-to-face interview. Perhaps this view [is] justified, because the two methods had many deficiencies and problems. Surveys by mail typically elicited extremely low response rates, even with short questionnaires. . . . Further, it was not possible to reach many people by mail questionnaires; among those to whom questionnaires could be delivered, the best educated were far more likely to respond. Even completed questionnaires left much to be desired. . . . It is not surprising, then, that users of the mail questionnaire treated response rates well below 50 percent as "acceptable" and explained away problems of data quality with disclaimers such as, "this is the best we can expect from a mail questionnaire" (Dillman, 1978, pp. 1–2).

Not unlike the situation with mail surveys in the 1970s, many questions and concerns exist about how to best conduct Internet surveys and whether they are, in fact, scientifically valid. If you substitute "Internet" for "mail" and substitute "mail" for "face-to-face" in the first sentence of the Dillman quotation, the statement will accurately reflect much of the criticism directed at Internet surveys today. Therefore, it may be wise to consider Internet surveys as an alternative to traditional mail and phone surveys. Nevertheless, Internet-based surveys do have advantages over more-traditional methods in certain applications, and the use of this medium will continue to expand.

Internet surveys currently are in vogue largely because of four popular assumptions about how they stack up against more-traditional survey mediums: (1) they are less time consuming; (2) they are just as good or better than more-traditional surveys; (3) they are much cheaper to conduct; and (4) they are easier to execute. However, these assumptions may or may not be true depending on the individual circumstances of the survey. Furthermore, with the hype surrounding the Web in recent years, researchers sometimes base their decision on whether or not to conduct Web surveys on something other than substantive information. Therefore, researchers need to recognize the current limitations of Internet surveys.

To this end, this report offers information for researchers who must make an informed decision on whether Internet surveys are appropriate for their needs. We base our recommendations on evidence from the literature,[2] our own experiences in conducting Web surveys, and our discussions with fellow Web survey researchers, including individuals at the U.S. Census Bureau and the U.S. Air Force Surveys Branch.

Chapter Two of this report contains general background information on conducting surveys; in particular, we discuss important issues that one must keep in mind when planning a survey. Chapter Three presents a literature review of Web and e-mail surveys. Chapter Four addresses how to decide what type of Web survey to conduct, while focusing on the distinction between probability and convenience sampling. Chapter Five provides guidelines for designing and implementing Web surveys. Chapter Six offers case studies, and Chapter Seven presents our conclusions.

---

[2]The references in this report provide a complete list of the literature used in this study. We also specifically recommend the following reading by topic area: practical survey implementation—American Association for Public Opinion Research (1997), Dillman (2000), Fowler (1993), and Groves (1989); Web survey implementation—Couper (2000) and Dillman (2000); Sampling—Cochran (1977), Henry (1990), and Kish (1965); Web resources—www.websm.org.

Chapter Two

BACKGROUND ON THE SURVEY PROCESS

In this chapter, we present an overview of the various aspects of the research survey process.[1] We emphasize that surveying should first be thought of as a process. We then discuss how the interaction with survey respondents can be divided into three distinct segments— contact mode, response mode, and follow-up mode. Next, we explain the crucial distinction between probability samples and convenience samples, and finally, we discuss important considerations in planning a survey: response rates, cost, timeliness, sources of error, and data quality. (The literature review in Chapter Three is structured along these same lines.)

THE SURVEY PROCESS AS A WHOLE: THE BASIC STEPS

In discussions on surveying, the focus is often incorrectly placed only on the survey instrument and how it is fielded to the survey sample, and not on the entire survey process. The entire process also includes defining the survey objectives, developing a sample frame,[2] specifying the strategy for data collection, and conducting the appropriate analyses. Dillman (1978) provided a formal framework for conducting effective mail surveys that has proven successful over the past two decades. This formal framework, which recognizes that the

---

[1]This chapter is directed primarily toward principal investigators without a background in survey methodology. Although survey researchers may already be familiar with much of the material, it may nevertheless provide a useful overview.

[2]A *sample frame* is a list of individuals from which a sample is drawn. Ideally, the sample frame covers the entire population, and any discrepancy between the frame and the entire population is called the *sample frame bias.*

entire process of fielding a survey is important to achieving acceptable response rates, ultimately resulted in the widespread acceptance of mail surveys as a respected research methodology.

The basic tenet of the *Total* (or *Tailored*) *Design Method* (TDM) (Dillman, 1978 and 2000) and *Total Survey Design* (TSD) (Fowler, 1993) is that the entire survey process is critical to success. Essentially, TDM and TSD suggest that a researcher should take a holistic approach to survey design by consciously considering all aspects of the survey process. In particular, TDM emphasizes that the survey process is part of a social interaction between the researcher and the survey respondent and stresses the importance of appropriately communicating the survey to the respondent. TSD recognizes the trade-offs that must be made between methodological rigor in the various components of the survey process and the attendant costs, with an eye to developing a survey that meets the needs of the research study while recognizing the survey's constraints. Some texts, such as Groves (1989), center on structuring the entire survey design process in order to balance total measurement error with cost.

Although a formal survey-process framework is as yet undefined for Internet surveys, the basic steps in the process should be the same as with any other survey medium:

1. Defining the survey objectives, including

- specifying the population of interest
- delineating the type of data to be collected
- determining the desired precision of the results.

2. Determining who will be sampled, including

- specifying the method of sample selection as either
    - probability-based or
    - convenience-based[3]

---

[3]In a *probability sample*, the probability with which an individual is selected into a sample can be computed. When the probability cannot be computed, the sample is

- creating a sampling frame (if necessary)
- selecting the sample.

3. Creating and testing the instrument, including

- choosing the response mode (mail, Web, or other)
- drafting the questions
- pretesting and revising the survey instrument.

4. Contacting respondents throughout the survey process by using the following:

- prenotification that the survey is coming
- postdelivery reminder and thank-you
- nonresponse follow-up for those who do not return the survey.

5. Data collection, data reduction, and analysis.

CONTACT, RESPONSE, AND FOLLOW-UP MODES

Interaction with survey respondents can be divided into three main components: contact, response, and follow-up. Each of these three components can be conducted in a different mode, that is, by telephone, mail, Web, or e-mail. For example, respondents may be contacted by U.S. mail to participate in a Web survey and the follow-up for nonrespondents may be conducted in yet another mode.

This sort of categorization is not found in the traditional literature because not very many different combinations can be formed with the two most commonly used traditional survey modes: mail and telephone. However, we have found this classification to be important in categorizing and describing the various ways the Internet can be used in the survey process, and it proved useful in our compiling an evidence table of the literature (see Appendix B).

---

called a *convenience sample* (it is more "convenient" to not have to worry about the ability to compute probabilities of selection).

Response modes can also be grouped according to whether they are interviewer-administered or self-administered; in-person and telephone surveys fall into the former category whereas mail and Internet surveys fall into the latter. Responses can also be collected using a single mode or via mixed modes in which respondents may initially be given a choice of response media or the type of media is sequenced as potential respondents are contacted repeatedly.

PROBABILITY AND CONVENIENCE SAMPLES

Survey sampling can be grouped into the following two broad categories: probability-based sampling (also loosely known as random sampling)[4] and convenience sampling. In this report, we concentrate much of our discussion on probability-based surveying because the probability selection mechanism allows for valid statistical inference about an entire population, which is often the focus of research surveys.

As stated earlier, a sample is considered a *probability sample* when the probability with which every person was selected into the sample is known. The sampling probabilities for each person are not necessarily equal. Oftentimes, the population can be enumerated in some fashion. This enumeration results in a list or some other mechanism from which individuals are selected. This enumeration may be an actual one (for example, a complete list of the population) or it may be implied (such as with a multistage sampling scheme in which only the members of selected primary sampling units are actually enumerated). Because probability samples are relatively expensive, probability-based surveys stand to benefit the most from less-costly survey alternatives becoming available through Internet-based surveying.

With a *convenience sample,* the probability by which every respondent was included in the sample cannot be determined. Generating convenience samples typically requires much less time and effort than generating probability samples, and thus usually involves less

---

[4]Some researchers use the term "random sampling" to describe only those samples that have equal probability of being selected. In this report, we employ the more-colloquial usage of the term random sampling.

cost, but convenience samples generally do not support statistical inference. Nevertheless, convenience sampling can be useful to researchers in a number of ways. For example, responses from a convenience sample might be useful in developing hypotheses early in the course of research, identifying various issues surrounding the research subject, defining response categories for multiple-response questions, or collecting other sorts of noninferential data. In fact, in certain types of qualitative research, convenience samples generated from the Web may be just as valid as convenience samples that are generated using other modes. Also, the advent of more-sophisticated statistical techniques, most notably propensity scoring[5] (Rosenbaum and Rubin, 1983 and 1984), may allow some types of inference from convenience samples.

We do not discuss survey sampling any further in this report, but details on survey sampling can be found in Kish (1965), Cochran (1977), and Henry (1990). In Chapter Four, we discuss various types of Internet surveys that arise from the distinction between probability and convenience samples.

IMPORTANT CONSIDERATIONS IN PLANNING A SURVEY

In this section, we point out the major considerations that drive the choice of mode or modes employed in the survey design process—particularly in a research survey. Later, we compare and contrast conventional and Internet-based alternatives.[6]

Response Rates

When methodological statements are made about surveys, it is the response rate that is often mentioned first. Response rates are measured relative to the size of the sampling frame and therefore are only as good as the sample frame itself. Any discrepancy between the sampling frame and the target population is referred to as *coverage*

---

[5]*Propensity scoring* is a technique that can be used to reduce the bias that arises when individuals are not probabilistically selected into a sample (so-called self-selection bias).

[6]For comprehensive texts on planning and conducting surveys, see Fowler (1993), Groves (1989), or Dillman (2000).

error. (This subject is covered in more detail later in the section "Sources of Error.")

Because there are no sampling frames for convenience samples, response rates for those samples are not meaningful. It may be interesting to report response rates when they can be computed, but they cannot be interpreted in the same way that response rates for probability samples are interpreted.

For the traditional response modes—including telephone, mail, and in-person—de Leeuw (1992) studied how survey mode affects responses, both in terms of response rates and biases. She classified mode factors into three categories: (1) media related (the visual presentation, for example); (2) information-transmission related (the telephone lines, for example); and (3) factors that affect the impact the interviewer has on the respondent. She found little difference among interviewer-assisted modes (in-person or telephone interviews) in terms of data quality (such as for item or unit nonresponse).[7] When comparing interviewer-assisted modes with mail, de Leeuw found that interviewer-assisted modes result in higher response rates and lower item nonresponse, but also tended to bias the answers toward ones that are more socially acceptable (de Leeuw, 1992, p. 118). That is, mail surveys were found to have higher item and unit nonresponse rates, but when questions *were* answered, the responses were of better quality, particularly for sensitive questions.

Cost

Designing a survey requires making trade-offs between the quality and quantity of data and the cost to obtain that data. Here, we provide a general comparison of costs for various survey alternatives, holding all other survey dimensions constant.

One component of total survey cost that is sometimes overlooked is the researchers' time for survey design and subsequent data analysis. This can be a major cost component depending on the size of the survey. However, the costs for design and data analysis vary little by

---

[7]*Item nonresponse* occurs when a respondent chooses not to respond to an individual question. *Unit nonresponse* occurs when a member of the sample does not participate in any part of the survey.

contact, response, or follow-up mode. One major expense that does vary by mode is the labor cost for personnel who actually execute the survey. Depending on the size of the survey and the complexity of its design, researcher labor costs or survey personnel labor costs, or a combination of the two, may end up being a significant portion of the survey budget.

Interviewer labor costs tend to make face-to-face surveys the most expensive to conduct, followed by telephone interview surveys. Mail surveys eliminate interviewer labor by substituting it with the less labor-intensive activities of assembling survey mail packages and coding the responses when they are returned.

Consider a survey that takes a respondent one-half hour to complete. For a face-to-face interview, the project will incur costs for the half-hour interview plus the interviewer's travel time to the interviewing location, which can often exceed the length of the interview. For the telephone interview, the project incurs only the half-hour cost for the actual interview time plus a lesser amount of time to arrange for the interview. For a mail survey, the project incurs a few minutes of labor time to assemble the survey package and mail it and, more important, a certain amount of time, depending on the length and complexity of the survey, for a coder and data-entry person to enter information from the completed paper surveys into an electronic database.

Therefore, the amount of interviewer time per survey tends to be greatest with the face-to-face mode, followed by the telephone mode, and then mail. Furthermore, the time differential tends to be compounded by an interviewer cost differential because face-to-face interviewers tend to be more highly compensated, followed by telephone interviewers, and finally by administrative people who prepare survey packages, code the completed questionnaires, and enter data.

Instrument costs, such as printing costs for face-to-face and mail surveys, CATI programming costs for telephone interviews, and postage costs for mail surveys, tend to be much smaller budgetary items, although they can vary according to the complexity of the instrument and the survey sample size. For a mail survey, the labor cost for one day of a researcher's time corresponds to the cost of mailing and printing of several hundred surveys, assuming printing and mailing costs of around three or four dollars per survey.

Timeliness

In today's increasingly fast-paced world, survey timeliness is becoming more heavily stressed. Surveys for public policy research tend to have such limited time horizons in which to affect policy that a mediocre survey completed at a critical point in time may be valued more than a good survey with later results.

The length of time required to field a survey is a function of the contact, response, and follow-up modes. Decreasing the time in one or more of these parts of the survey process tends to decrease the overall time spent in the field. However, it is important to keep in mind that the relevant measure is not the average response time but the *maximum* response time (or a large percentile of the response time distribution) because survey analysis will not begin until all (or most) of the responses are in.

For conventional survey modes, the telephone provides the fastest response, followed generally by mail, and then face-to-face interviews. It is difficult to quantify the time it takes to field each mode because that time period is a function of the size of the particular survey sample and the amount of available resources (such as the number of interviewers). Some time-difference comparisons can be made, however. First, all of the conventional modes require increasing resources as the sample size increases. For interviewer-assisted modes, a direct connection exists between the number of interviewers and the rate at which surveys can be completed. For self-administered (conventional) surveys, the main resource constraint is the number of personnel available to transcribe the paper-based responses into an electronic format.

Second, limitations in these resources will result in a relatively long fielding period (the time period during which respondents are allowed to respond to a survey). For the interviewer-assisted modes, the availability of interviewer resources drives the survey completion rate, which, in turn, dictates the length of the fielding period. Generally speaking, the longer the fielding period, the fewer the number of interviewers need be trained because the interview work can be spread out over time, which is cost-effective. For the average mail survey, the length of time required for postal mail delivery of the initial instrument and its subsequent return, compounded with at least a second iteration for nonresponse, dictates a fielding period of at least weeks, and more likely months, in length.

Sources of Error

The primary purpose of a survey is to gather information about a population group. Even when a survey is conducted as a census,[8] the results can be affected by several potential sources of error, as we explain later in this chapter. A good survey design seeks to reduce all types of possible errors, and not just the sampling errors arising from surveying only a part of the population.

Survey error is commonly characterized in terms of the precision of the statistical estimates. However, characterizing survey error only in terms of standard errors and response rates ignores other ways in which errors can enter the survey process.

Table 2.1 lists the four general categories of sources of survey error, as defined in Groves (1989) as part of his "Total Survey Error" approach (we recommend Groves for those interested in exploring this topic in greater detail).

Coverage errors occur when some part of the population of interest cannot become part of the sample. Groves (1989) specifies four different types of populations:

1. The *population of inference* is the population about which the researcher ultimately intends to draw conclusions.

2. The *target population* is the population of inference minus various groups that the researcher has chosen to disregard.

3. The *frame population* is that portion of the target population that can be enumerated via a sampling frame.

---

[8]In a *census,* the entire population is surveyed. With a sample, only a subset of the population is surveyed.

Table 2.1

Types of Survey Errors and Their Source

Error	Source
Coverage	Failure to give any chance of sample selection to some individuals in the population
Sampling	Heterogeneity in the survey measure among persons in the population
Nonresponse	Failure to collect data on all persons in the sample
Measurement	Inaccuracies in responses recorded on the survey instruments that arise from: • The effect interviewers have on respondents' answers to survey questions • Respondent error (from the respondent's inability to answer questions, lack of requisite effort to obtain the correct answer, or other psychological factors) • Error due to the weakness in the wording of survey questionnaires • Error due to effects of the mode of data collection (such as face-to-face or telephone communications).

SOURCE: Groves (1989).

4. The *survey sample* consists of those members of the sampling frame who were chosen to be surveyed.

Coverage error, then, is generally defined as the difference between the statistics calculated on the frame population and on the target population. The two most common approaches to reducing coverage error are (1) obtaining as complete a sampling frame as possible and (2) post-stratifying to weight the survey sample to match the population of inference on some key characteristics. In some cases, it is also possible to employ a "frameless" sampling strategy that, when properly designed, may allow every member of the target population a positive chance to be sampled.

For surveys conducted over the Internet, there is the concern that a large fraction of the general population does not have access to a personal computer or is otherwise unable to participate in an Internet-based survey. Just as telephone surveys were less effective when phone technology was new and telephone service was not widespread, surveying via the Internet today excludes a significant portion of the U.S. population.

Furthermore, in the case of Internet surveys, access is not the only issue affecting coverage. Even if respondents do have access to the Internet (for example, through a public library), they may be computer illiterate and would have difficulty in correctly responding to an on-line survey. Just as it would be ineffective to survey a functionally illiterate group of people using a paper-based survey, it is ineffective to use the Internet to survey those who lack computer literacy. In addition to access and computer know-how, respondents must also have compatible hardware and software in order to successfully complete an Internet survey.

To make a crude analogy with telephone surveys, imagine if only 50 percent of the population were accessible by telephone and, of that 50 percent, some are unable to answer the phones they do have and others have phones that are incompatible with the caller's phone. Until Internet communication becomes as commonplace as telephone calling, evaluating a target population's ability to participate will always be a major factor in the relative success of an Internet-based survey.

Sampling errors arise when only a subset of the target population is surveyed yet inference is made about the whole population. Assuming that no difference exists between the population of inference and the target population, the sampling error is simply a quantification of the uncertainty in the sample statistic. This uncertainty can be divided into a variance component and a bias component. Groves (1989) stated that *variance* characterizes the variability in the sample statistic that arises from the heterogeneity on the survey measure (or estimate) among the population. In other words, variance characterizes the variability of an estimate that stems from the fact that drawing a different sample will result in a different estimate. *Bias,* on the other hand, is the systematic difference between the sample statistic and the actual population parameter of interest.

When thinking most simply about the precision of statistical estimates that are drawn through probabilistic sampling mechanisms, such estimates are improved by larger sample sizes, which can be achieved by either selecting a larger sample of potential respondents to begin with or minimizing nonresponse through various mechanisms, or by a combination of both approaches.

In the absence of significant nonresponse, the probabilistic sampling mechanism is assumed to minimize the possibility of bias. Convenience sampling, on the other hand, is generally assumed to result in biased samples because the mechanism that generated the sample is not understood (that is, the probability with which an individual is selected into the sample is not known). Convenience sampling frequently is undertaken because it is either too difficult or too costly to create a sampling frame.

Nonresponse errors occur when individual respondents do not participate in any part of the survey (unit nonresponse) or respondents do not answer individual survey questions (item nonresponse). Groves (1989) stated that "nonresponse is an error of nonobservation." The response rate, which is the ratio of the number of respondents to the number sampled, is often taken as a measure of goodness. Higher response rates limit the severity of the nonresponse bias. We discuss nonresponse more fully in the next section.

Measurement errors arise when the survey response differs from the "true" response. For example, respondents may not answer sensitive questions honestly for a variety of reasons, or respondents may make errors in answering questions or misinterpret the questions posed to them. These measurement errors may be mitigated, or exacerbated, by the mode of data collection. We discuss this more fully in the next section.

Data Quality

Data quality can be judged along a number of lines: (1) low unit and item nonresponse; (2) honesty of responses, particularly for questions of a sensitive nature; (3) completeness of responses, particularly for open-ended questions; and, (4) low error rate in transcription into an electronic format for analysis, when required by the response mode.

Response rates may be easy to calculate,[9] but the most important issue in data quality is the extent to which nonrespondents would have

---

[9]Note, however, that response rate is an imperfect measure as it usually does not take into account sampling weights.

responded differently than respondents. If ancillary information about nonrespondents and respondents is known, survey weights can be adjusted to account for the nonresponse. However, if the statistic of interest is imperfectly related to the ancillary information, then the resulting adjustment may not completely or appropriately correct the bias that occurs from the nonresponse. The response rate becomes increasingly important as one anticipates that a difference between the sample and the population exists with respect to the statistics of interest.

With all other factors, such as prenotification and nonresponse follow-up, held constant, unit and item nonresponse are generally smaller when using interviewer-assisted modes (de Leeuw, 1992) than when using self-administered survey modes, although the interviewer-assisted modes tend to be more expensive. Face-to-face interviews have long been considered the gold standard of surveys. They tend to result in the lowest unit and item nonresponse and minimize respondents' misinterpretation of questions.

It has been shown that interviewer-administered survey modes, particularly face-to-face ones, yield answers that are more socially acceptable than do self-administered modes (de Leeuw, 1992; Kiesler and Sproull, 1986, p. 409). This is particularly relevant for surveys on sensitive topics or for surveys that contain sensitive questions, such as those regarding personal income or sexual practices.

Telephone surveys offer many of the advantages of face-to-face surveys at a lower cost. However, they suffer from higher unit nonresponse and have the same difficulties of bias toward socially acceptable responses to sensitive questions. It is frequently difficult to solicit long responses to open-ended questions over the telephone and respondents find it more difficult to understand and respond to complex questions or questions with complex response sets.

Mail and other self-administered modes tend to be the least expensive to use but often have higher unit and item nonresponse rates. On the other hand, they tend to elicit the most-accurate responses to sensitive questions.

One concluding point of interest: The quality of data transcription is an issue with conventional surveys because all conventional surveys require some form of conversion into an electronic format for analysis. With Internet surveys, however, the answers that respondents enter into an on-line form oftentimes can be directly downloaded into a database, thereby avoiding transcription errors.

Chapter Three

LITERATURE REVIEW OF WEB AND E-MAIL SURVEYS

In this chapter, we examine what has been written about Internet surveys in the literature, specifically Web and e-mail surveys. We address the topics of response rate, cost, timeliness, sources of error, and data quality.[1] We compare two conventional survey modes, mail and telephone, with Internet survey modes. The other widely used conventional mode, face-to-face interviewing, is not addressed here because little has been written about it in comparison with Web and e-mail surveys given the high cost of in-person interviewing.[2]

A BRIEF HISTORY OF ELECTRONIC SURVEYS

Beginning in the late 1980s and early 1990s, prior to the widespread use of the Web, e-mail was explored as a survey mode.[3] As with the Web today, e-mail offered the possibility of nearly instantaneous transmission of surveys at little or no cost. Unlike the Web, however, early e-mail was essentially static, consisting of a basic ASCII (text-

---

[1]The literature contains far more information about response rates than about any other topic related to surveying, such as timeliness or data quality. Appendix B contains a more detailed discussion of response rates in the literature and Appendix C lists the survey topic, sample size, type of sample, contact/response/follow-up mode, and response rate for each study referenced in this report.

[2]We do not address other electronic survey modes that are currently in use, such as computerized self-administered questionnaires (CSAQs), which are surveys distributed via computer diskette. Two other electronic modes, CAPI and CATI, as we noted earlier, are unrelated to the development of the Internet and therefore we do not discuss them in this report.

[3]It is worth noting that the survey literature as late as the early- to mid-1990s could not anticipate the eventual influence of the Web on the practice of surveying.

only) message that was delivered via the Internet.[4] E-mail surveys tended to resemble the linear structure of a paper survey and were generally limited in length. Furthermore, because e-mail surveys were primarily text-based, document formatting was rudimentary at best. The only significant advantage they offered over paper surveys was a potential decrease in delivery and response time and cost, although some observers also hypothesized that the novelty of the new medium might actually have enhanced response rates (Parker, 1992; Zhang, 2000).

The Web started to become widely available in the early- to mid-1990s and quickly supplanted e-mail as the Internet survey medium of choice. Whereas early e-mail was all ASCII-based, the Web offered the possibility of multimedia surveys containing audio and video, as well as an enhanced user interface and more interactive features. For convenience samples, the Web also offered a way around the necessity of having to know respondents' e-mail addresses.

RESPONSE RATES OF INTERNET SURVEYS

Response rates for Internet surveys in the literature are summarized graphically in Figure 3.1 by survey mode (more-exact numbers can be found in Appendix B). Overall, Figure 3.1 suggests that surveys using a mail response mode and surveys using both a mail and Web response mode tend to have higher response rates than those using just an e-mail or Web response mode.

Response rates range from 7 to 44 percent for Web surveys and from 6 to 68 percent for e-mail surveys. Some studies in the literature gave respondents the choice of responding by either mail or via the Web. Of the seven studies we examined, five reported that respondents

---

[4]Since the early days of e-mail, the ability to send attachments and executable files with e-mail has greatly expanded. Today, e-mail can be used to send a survey program to a user to run on his or her computer. The user can then return the completed survey electronically or by mail. These CSAQ surveys can be delivered via a number of different types of media, including e-mail attachments, downloading from the Web, or via diskette or CD-ROM.

RAND*MR1480-3.1*

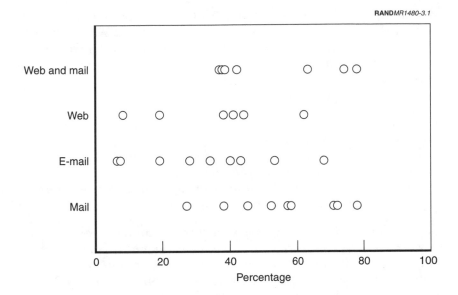

**Figure 3.1—Response Rates for Internet Surveys in the Literature,
by Survey Mode**

more often chose to respond by mail than through the Web and two
studies found just the reverse. Above all else, the context of the
individual study seems to matter. For example, respondents for the
study with the highest percentage of Web respondents were
recruited through advertising in Internet discussion groups (Schleyer
and Forrest, 2000).

Several studies in the literature involve conducting experiments to
determine whether e-mail surveys have lower or higher response
rates than postal mail surveys. In such studies, identical questionnaires were sent to different portions (or study arms) of the same
population. The only difference between the study arms was in
whether the respondent was asked to respond via e-mail or by mail.
In most studies, the mail response rate was higher by as much as 21
percent. Only one study resulted in a lower mail response rate.
However, that study was in many respects unusual and fell at a time
when the novelty of e-mail may have influenced the results (Parker,
1992).

In one experiment (Quigley et al., 2000), it was reported that a mail response option needed to be used in addition to a Web response option because response rates were unacceptably low. The same authors also mention that giving respondents the option of requesting a mail survey (rather than mailing it out to everyone) proved unsuccessful because few respondents took advantage of the option.

For a number of studies, survey participants were recruited through advertising in newsgroups, on Web pages, or in newspapers. It is not possible to compute a response rate for these studies. Moreover, these samples constitute convenience samples. As we mentioned previously, response rates for convenience samples may be interesting, but they are not scientifically meaningful.

Several commercial enterprises specialize in conducting Web surveys. Knowledge Networks (www.knowledgenetworks.com) and Harris Interactive (www.harrisinteractive.com) are the most prominent ones. However, the two firms use completely different approaches to fielding surveys via the Internet.

Knowledge Networks recruits panels of individuals via random digit dialing (RDD) to participate in ongoing surveys. Although Knowledge Networks does offer researchers a probability sample, the overall response rate averages only 25 to 30 percent.[5] In addition, Knowledge Networks gives researchers the option of surveying panel nonrespondents over the telephone, which increases the overall response rate to about 40 to 50 percent (Dennis, 2001) but of course also increases the cost.

A special feature of Knowledge Networks is that it installs the requisite hardware (WebTV) in respondents' homes at no charge and assumes the monthly service costs so that respondents can fill out the

---

[5]On average, 56 percent of the initially contacted households agree to join a panel. Of those, 72 percent allow the required WebTV hardware to be installed. Of that portion, 83 percent complete the core survey that makes them eligible for filling out future surveys. The average response rate for a Knowledge Networks Web survey is 75 percent, which yields an overall average response rate of 25 percent (Berrens et al., 2001). Mike Dennis, Knowledge Networks' vice president of government and academic relations, said that more-recent numbers are higher: The initial contact rate is unchanged, the hardware installation rate is 80 percent, the core survey completion rate is 88 percent, and the survey response rate is 75 to 85 percent. Combined, these numbers yield an overall response rate between 30 and 33 percent.

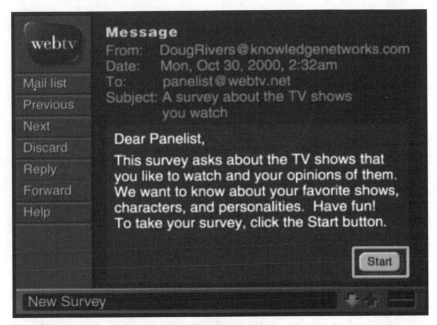

Screen shot courtesy of Knowledge Networks.

Figure 3.2—Knowledge Networks' WebTV Survey Invitation

surveys using their television sets. Figure 3.2 shows a WebTV screen shot inviting panelists to participate in a survey. Providing respondents with hardware, software, and other connectivity requirements allows Knowledge Networks to reach a broader cross-section of the population than would otherwise be possible.

Knowledge Networks' panels are similar in spirit to Nielsen survey panels used to determine television ratings. Knowledge Networks survey panelists receive three or four surveys a month, each requiring 10 to 15 minutes to complete. Sampling is controlled so that the panelists do not receive more than one survey on a given topic in a three-month period. As of August 2001, Knowledge Networks had more than 200,000 panelists enrolled, or approximately 80,000 households. The company claims that it adds about 5,000 panelists per month and projects an eventual total panel size of 250,000.

Harris Interactive constructed and maintains a database of several million volunteer Web survey participants. The volunteers are recruited from a variety of sources including advertising on the Internet. Because they volunteer to be part of Harris's panel, the participants are self-selected. For any particular survey effort, a sample from the Harris panel database is asked to participate.

To generalize its survey results, Harris Interactive uses a statistical methodology called *propensity scoring* to re-weight the estimates based on the convenience sample. Propensity scoring was invented to deal with selection bias,[6] but has not traditionally been used in the context of surveys. (We present a case study in Chapter Six that involves propensity scoring.)

COST OF A WEB SURVEY VERSUS OTHER MODES

Assessing the cost of doing a Web survey versus mail or some other survey mode is difficult because different writers on the subject have defined costs in different ways. Cost estimates vary depending on whether they are given relative to the number of mail-outs or relative to the number of completed survey responses and, unfortunately, most studies in the literature omit any discussion about costs altogether. Nevertheless, the question of cost often comes down to how to best price the time spent programming a Web survey, and whether and how to price the investigator or survey coordinator's time because marginal personnel costs are almost always significantly greater than any other marginal survey cost (such as printing and postage).

Although lower costs are often touted as one of the benefits of Internet surveys, Couper et al. (1999) found no cost benefit with e-mail surveys as compared with postal-mail surveys. In a large and comprehensive survey of various government agencies, Couper et al. compared an all-e-mail survey (contact, response, and follow-up) with an all-postal-mail survey. They found that evaluating and testing the e-mail software took more than 150 hours—almost four

---

[6]Propensity scoring is not a panacea for all selection bias. It can only adjust for so-called ignorable bias. ("Ignorable" bias is more important than the name suggests.) For more details, see Rosenbaum and Rubin (1983).

times what they had budgeted. For the postal mail survey, costs for printing and postage were $1.60 per reply, and data editing and entry costs came to $1.81 per reply. For the e-mail survey, managing the e-mail itself cost $1.74 per completed case. In addition, in the Couper et al. study, more than 900 toll-free calls of a mostly technical nature were handled. Although the printing and mailing costs were eliminated for the e-mail survey, Couper et al. found that the cost of evaluating and testing the e-mail software, additional post-collection processing,[7] and maintaining a toll-free phone line (largely dedicated to responding to technical questions related to the e-mail surveys) offset any savings.

Another team of researchers, Schleyer and Forrest (2000), received survey responses over the Web and by postal mail and fax. Their costs included programming a 22-item survey in HTML (hypertext markup language) and in Perl, a high-level programming language (35 hours at $30 an hour); software testing (eight hours at $60 an hour); operating a bulk-mailer program (three hours at $60 an hour); and manual entry of some Web surveys ($206 total). An equivalent calculation was done for a postal mail survey, based on $1.45 per mailing and $4 for data entry per 22-item survey. Schleyer and Forrest found that the total costs for the Web survey turned out to be 38 percent lower than for the equivalent mail survey. A break-even calculation shows that a Web survey would be more economical than a postal mail survey when more than 347 people respond; the reverse is true with less than 189 responses. When the number of responses runs between 189 and 347, it is unclear which mode would turn out to be more economical.

Asch (2001) found that adding a Web response option to a mail survey was economical when about 580 responses are obtained over the Web and when the Web is used as the primary response mode and surveys are mailed out to nonrespondents only. The calculations are based on the trade-off from the expected savings in postage, printing, and labor costs to prepare survey mailing packages and code the subsequent survey returns against the expected additional

---

[7]The e-mail survey was designed so that respondents would use the reply function of their e-mail program. If done properly, the resulting reply could have been automatically read into a database upon receipt. However, almost 47 percent of the e-mail surveys required some type of clerical action to prepare them for automatic reading.

costs of programming, additional management effort, and maintaining a telephone help line for the Web survey. Asch's study did realize cost savings because it secured more than 1,000 Web responses.

In two studies that essentially disregard personnel costs, Mehta and Sivadas (1995) and Jones and Pitt (1999), the authors concluded that Internet-based surveys are less costly than mail surveys. These conclusions simply stem from the fact that Internet surveys do not incur postage and printing costs whereas postal mail surveys do. Mehta and Sivadas compared an e-mail survey to two forms of mail response surveys and concluded that the two postal mail surveys had "minimum costs" of $0.58 and $2.16 per mail out. This cost calculation reflects only the cost for postage in the first case and costs for postage and an additional dollar incentive in the second case. Jones and Pitt reported on a study with three arms: e-mail only, e-mail and Web, and postal mail. They reported the costs to be 35 pence, 41 pence, and 92 pence per reply, respectively.[8] These costs reflect the mailing costs in Great Britain and a marginal labor cost of six British pounds per hour.

For a typical survey, Knowledge Networks currently charges around $35 per completed survey with a survey questionnaire that takes about 10 to 12 minutes to complete.[9] A large number of additional demographic and other variables are available from the Knowledge Networks core survey[10] at no extra charge.

In conclusion, when considering only postage and printing costs, e-mail and Web surveys appear to cheaper than postal mail surveys. In actuality, it appears that Web surveys become more economical than postal mail surveys only when the number of responses reaches a certain threshold—somewhere between a few hundred and a thousand. However, unanticipated technical problems are likely to arise when researchers have no prior experience with Web survey

---

[8]A British pound is worth 100 pence. At the time of this writing, one pound was worth $1.45 in U.S. dollars.

[9]The price varies substantially depending upon the scale of the project and the amount of subsampling and screening required for identifying the target population.

[10]Knowledge Networks requires each respondent to fill out a core survey before he or she responds to the main survey. This avoids having to include standardized questions in every survey.

programming, and these problems can easily eliminate all potential cost benefits.

COMPARING SPEED AND TIMELINESS OF INTERNET SURVEYS WITH OTHER MODES

Most studies have concluded, often with little or no empirical evidence to back up the conclusion, that Internet-based surveys are conducted more quickly than surveys sent by postal mail. This conclusion is usually based on the fact that e-mail and other forms of online communication can be instantaneously transmitted whereas postal mail must be physically delivered, which of course takes more time. However, a blanket conclusion that Internet surveys are faster than mail surveys naively ignores the reality that the total amount of time for survey fielding includes more than just the survey response time.

A total comparison must take into account the mode of contact and how long the process takes, in addition to the follow-up mode and potential multiple follow-up contact periods. For example, if the respondents' e-mail addresses are unavailable and a probability sample is desired, respondents may then have to be contacted by mail. In this case, the Web survey saves time only for the return delivery of the completed questionnaire, and not for the contact and follow-up, so the resulting time savings may be only a fraction of the total survey fielding time.

In the case of e-mail surveys, where the presumption is that the potential respondents' e-mail addresses are known and, therefore, can be used not just for delivering the survey but also for prenotification and nonresponse follow-up, the time savings can be substantial. For example, allowing for a week of delivery time with postal mail is not uncommon. With an advance letter and just a single mail follow-up, this one-week delay can telescope into a month in survey fielding time. Two weeks must then be budgeted for initial survey delivery and return time, plus an additional two weeks for delivery and response on a single follow-up reminder. In comparison, with an all-electronic process, the same operations could potentially be completed in a few days or less.

Yet, even in an all-Internet environment, it is not necessarily true that the Internet-based survey will be more timely. For example, in a comparison of response speeds with e-mail and postal mail, Tse et al. (1995) did not find a statistically significant difference in the time between delivery and receipt of a survey sent by e-mail and an equivalent survey sent by postal mail to university faculty and staff.[11] Furthermore, to achieve sufficiently high response rates, it may be necessary to keep an Internet survey in the field for an extended period of time. For example, Knowledge Networks has said that to achieve 70 to 80 percent response rates,[12] it must leave a survey in the field for about ten days. This period of time comprises one workweek with two weekends because Knowledge Networks has found that most respondents complete their surveys over the weekend.

There are, however, cases in the literature that do show more-timely response rates. Tse (1998) found a statistically significant difference in the average *initial* response time for those who received an e-mail survey versus those who received a paper survey through their university's campus mail (one day versus two-and-a-half). Further, in Tse's experiment, most e-mail survey recipients either responded almost immediately (within one day) or they did not respond at all, which raises the question of the effectiveness of nonresponse follow-up in the electronic forum. Schaefer and Dillman (1998) also document faster response rates with e-mail: From the day they sent out survey questionnaires, it took on average of 9.16 days to receive the questionnaires by e-mail versus an average of 14.39 days by postal mail.

A final note: Commercial survey firms that use prerecruited panels of volunteers can execute Web surveys extremely quickly (see Chapter Four).

---

[11]Although not statistically significant, the e-mail survey had a mean response time of just over eight days, while the equivalent mail survey had a mean response of almost ten days.

[12]The response rate refers to the number of people who received a particular survey. When factoring in various other forms of nonresponse, this rate declines to about 25 to 30 percent.

SOURCES OF ERROR WITH INTERNET SURVEYS

Coverage error is the most widely recognized shortcoming of Internet surveys. Although the fraction of the population with Internet access and the skills and hardware necessary to use the Web is continually increasing, the general population coverage for Internet-based surveys still lags considerably behind the coverage achievable using conventional survey modes. But, there are some important caveats to keep in mind.

First, the coverage differential is rapidly decreasing and may become immaterial in the near future. Second, even though conventional survey modes provide the ability to reach most of the survey population, getting people to respond is becoming increasingly difficult (for example, caller ID and answering machines are routinely used to screen calls from telephone surveyors and solicitors). Third, whereas conventional modes have near universal coverage, there will always be special subpopulations that have little or no coverage with any mode. Finally, a population with less-than-universal access to the Internet can be immaterial for some studies, such as those that focus on closed populations with equivalent access or populations of Internet users.

To improve coverage, Dillman (2000) recommends a dual-mode strategy for contact—using both e-mail and postal mail for pre-notification. Similarly, using dual-response modes, such as Web and e-mail, can be used to increase coverage.

Sampling error issues with Internet surveys are generally the same as those with conventional surveys. However, as the Internet expands, collecting much larger samples becomes more feasible. In fact, we recently talked to individuals at some organizations whose entire survey populations have electronic access; these organizations are considering eliminating sampling altogether and conducting just censuses. Often, these census efforts result in much larger numbers of respondents than otherwise could have been gathered using traditional survey sampling techniques and those larger numbers give the appearance of greater statistical accuracy. However, such accuracy may be misleading if nonresponse biases are not accounted for. Researchers need to carefully consider the trade-off between smaller samples that allow for careful nonresponse follow-up and larger samples with limited or no nonresponse follow-up. Smaller samples may result in larger standard errors but less bias, whereas the larger samples may result in much smaller standard errors but an unknown amount of bias.

Debates over whether certain sampling frames and sampling methodologies are appropriate for a given research question are not unique to Internet-based surveys.[13] Similar issues exist with conventional survey methods as well, although the inevitable decisions that must be made with respect to managing costs often require researchers to carefully weigh the pros and cons of one sampling method over another. With Internet-based surveys, it is easy to overlook these issues because the marginal cost of doing a census versus a sample *seems* to be small.

Finally, Web surveys clearly offer the opportunity to improve on other forms of self-administered surveys in terms of data validation, *skip pattern* automation,[14] and elimination of transcription errors, all of which help to minimize measurement error. Web surveys can be programmed to conduct input validation as a logical check of respondents' answers. These types of checks improve data quality and subsequently save time in the preparation of the analysis file.

Although the possibility of programming errors exists, automation of skip patterns eliminates the possibility that a respondent may skip to the wrong question. From the respondent's point of view, skip pattern automation also simplifies the process of taking the survey. And, whereas all conventional surveys require some form of conversion into an electronic format for analysis, with Web surveys, the respon-

---

[13]For example, a continuing debate in preelection polling is whether it is better to sample from existing voter registration lists or use RDD. The former excludes those not currently registered that might later register and the latter is known to result in, sometimes significant, overreporting of voting behavior. The choice, of course, depends on the particular research question (see Larson, 2001).

[14]A *skip pattern* refers to a respondent taking an alternative path through a questionnaire depending on his or her answer to an earlier question. For example, if a respondent answers that he or she is a renter rather than a homeowner, then the skip pattern would direct the respondent to skip past the questions related to mortgage payments.

dents' answers are directly downloaded into a database, thus avoiding transcription errors.

DATA QUALITY IN E-MAIL VERSUS MAIL SURVEYS

Data quality is usually measured by the number of respondents who have, intentionally or unintentionally, missed at least one survey item or by the percentage of missed items on respondents' questionnaires. For open-ended questions, longer answers are usually considered to be more informative and of higher quality. For closed-ended questions, it appears that e-mail surveys may incur a higher percentage of missed items than do postal mail surveys. As Table 3.1 shows, postal mail respondents on average miss fewer than 1 percent of survey items whereas e-mail respondents miss from 0.3 to 3.7 percent of survey items.

Paolo et al. (2000) also found that 27 percent of e-mail respondents did not respond to at least one question versus 9 percent of mail respondents that did the same. Kiesler and Sproull (1986) found the opposite: In their e-mail (contact and response) study arm, only 10 percent of respondents failed to complete or had spoiled one item, compared with 22 percent in the mail (contact and response) study arm. Tse (1998) and Tse et al. (1995) found no difference in the quality of responses from postal mail and e-mail survey respondents.

For open-ended questions, the literature shows that e-mail responses are either longer than or the same length as mail responses. Comley (1996) found that for two open-ended questions, e-mail respondents gave longer answers than did mail respondents. (One e-mail respondent in the Comley study wrote what amounted to a mini-essay.) Mehta and Sivadas (1995, p. 436) found "hardly any difference" between the average completed mail and e-mail responses for both open and close-ended questions. Across all survey arms in the Mehta and Sivadas study, 95 percent of respondents completed the one open-ended question as compared with an average of 98 percent of respondents who completed the close-ended question. Kiesler and Sproull (1986) found that the total number of words written by e-mail respondents as compared with mail respondents did not significantly differ. If one takes into account that open-ended items for mail respondents are not always encoded for cost reasons,

Table 3.1

Average Percentage of Missed Items for E-mail and Postal Mail Surveys

Study	E-mail	Postal Mail	Population
Bachman et al. (1996)	3.7	0.7	Business school deans and chairpersons
Comley (1996)[a]	1.2	0.4	Names and addresses purchased from Internet magazine in the UK
Paolo et al. (2000)	1.2	0.5	Fourth-year medical students
Couper et al. (1999)[b]	0.8	0.8	Employees of five U.S. federal agencies
Mehta and Sivadas (1995)[c]	< 0.3	< 0.3	Active U.S. users of bulletin board system (BBS) news group

[a] Based on three questions.

[b] Based on 81 attitude questions.

[c] Across five different study arms, one of which allowed for both mail and e-mail responses.

it would seem that Internet-based response modes are well suited to open-ended questions.

Finally, Walsh et al. (1992) report that self-selected respondents give higher-quality responses than randomly selected respondents, as might be expected. Open-ended responses from self-selected respondents were lengthier that those from randomly selected respondents, and self-selected respondents missed an average of 5 percent of closed-ended questions versus randomly selected respondents who missed an average of 12 percent.

Chapter Four

CHOOSING AMONG THE VARIOUS TYPES OF INTERNET SURVEYS

Here, we examine the various types of Internet surveys and the differences among them that factor into deciding what sort of survey is most appropriate for a particular study. At the heart of this decision lies the question of whether a researcher wants to make inferences about some larger population. This chapter deals with the consequences that arise from the answer to that question. (For instance, probability samples generally allow for inferences beyond the sample at hand, whereas convenience samples generally do not.)

Table 4.1 presents the various sampling selection methods related to Internet surveys for the two sampling categories. Later, we discuss each method in some detail.[1]

CONVENIENCE SAMPLING APPROACHES

Convenience sampling is characterized by a nonsystematic approach to recruiting respondents that often allows a potential respondent to self-select into the sample. Any sample in which the probability of a sample member's inclusion in the sample cannot be computed is considered to be a convenience sample. As we noted earlier in this report, convenience samples often require much less time and effort

---

[1]Other such taxonomies and further discussions on this topic can be found in Couper (2000) and Bradley (1999).

Table 4.1

Sampling Selection Methods for Internet-Based Surveys

Sampling Category	Selection Method
Convenience	Uncontrolled instrument distribution
	Systematic sampling of Web site visitors
	Volunteer panel
Probability	Sample from a closed population list
	Sample from a general population
	Prerecruited panel

to generate than probability samples, and thus are usually less costly. However, statistical inference is much more problematic with convenience samples. For example, in a survey about the environment, respondents who have an active interest in environmental issues may be more likely to self-select into the survey than others. Such a survey would likely overestimate the degree of concern within the general population about the environment.

Nevertheless, convenience sampling can be useful in other ways (as discussed in Chapter Two). It can be extremely valuable for hard-to-reach (although electronically connected) populations. Under certain assumptions, convenience samples can also be used for *model-based inference.*[2] In such a case, it is assumed that the regression model is correctly specified, meaning that all variables that affect the response are included in the model. Generally, a solid theory of how a model should be specified is not available and therefore variable selection procedures are employed. Moreover, it is possible to only disprove, and not prove, such a theory. Therefore, the assumption that the regression model is correctly specified is problematic.

Convenience samples are particularly unsuitable for estimating totals and fractions, which is often desirable in survey sampling.

---

[2]Although model-based inference is often employed in other branches of statistics, it remains controversial among survey statisticians. This may be due to historical developments specific to survey statistics.

Uncontrolled Instrument Distribution

By way of definition, a simple example of an uncontrolled instrument distribution is the posting of a survey on the Web for anyone to fill out. This type of Web survey has become ubiquitous. Certain organizations, including those supplying the daily news, routinely conduct Web polls, ostensibly for the reader's entertainment, and some Web sites exist for no other reason than to host polls (for example, misterpoll.com and survey.net). Participation in these surveys is entirely voluntary and self-selected. Chapter Six contains a case study that illustrates the use of an inexpensive survey with a convenience sample.

Surveys conducted via uncontrolled instrument distribution are "uncontrolled" because anyone with Web access can fill them out, as many times as they desire. There are ways to try to control multiple access by a particular computer user, but savvy users can fairly easily circumvent those safeguards. Similarly, screening questions can be implemented to prevent multiple access by the same individual. Preventing multiple access, however, does not change the fact that the sample constitutes a convenience sample.

In addition, survey sponsors can actively advertise their surveys in various venues in an attempt to encourage survey participation. Web advertising may be used to attract particular types of survey respondents, such as visitors to certain newsgroups or Web sites, just as commercial advertising might be used to attract specific types of consumers. But because the advertised survey cannot be restricted to solely the advertisement recipients, the distribution is still uncontrolled because anyone can have access to it. For an example of a Web survey using advertising, see Schillewaert et al. (1998).

Many uncontrolled instrument distribution surveys are published only on the Web or in newspaper articles. One exception is Coomber (1997), who conducted a survey of drug dealers worldwide. Coomber was interested in the practice of drug dilution (cutting drugs with other substances to increase profits). Specifically, he wanted to find out how common the practice of *dangerous* drug dilution (cutting drugs with substances such as household cleansers) was internationally. Obviously, lists of illegal drug dealers do not exist and therefore Coomber could not construct a sample frame. Instead,

Coomber advertised on newsgroups and directed respondents to a Web survey site. He also sent e-mails to individuals who had posted messages on the newsgroups. (To avoid being subpoenaed to reveal the respondents' e-mail addresses, Coomber did not attempt to learn their identities.) He recommended that respondents access the Web from a public terminal, such as one at a public library, or print the survey out and return it anonymously by postal mail. Coomber received 80 responses from 14 countries on four continents; 40 percent of the responses came from the United States.

Systematic Sampling of Web Site Visitors

Sampling every *nth* person from a sample frame that is ordered in some way is called *systematic sampling*. For instance, it is possible to have surveys "pop up" on the computer screen of every nth visitor to a Web site. One company, Zoomerang (www.zoomerang.com), sells technology that makes it possible to invite only every nth visitor to a site to fill out a survey.

Sampling every nth visitor constitutes a probability sample if one defines the target population as "visitors to this particular Web site." For other target populations, the outcome would be regarded as a convenience sample. In addition, cookies (small pieces of information stored on a Web users' computer) can be used to ensure that Web site visitors are selected to participate in a survey only once (assuming the user's Web browser accepts cookies).

Volunteer Panel

The *volunteer panel* method relies on assembling a group of individuals who have volunteered to participate in future surveys. The individuals are generally recruited into the panel through some form of advertising. Harris Interactive (see Chapter Three) employs a volunteer panel with a database of several million volunteer Web survey participants who were recruited from a variety of sources, including advertising on the Internet. Harris Interactive then conducts surveys using convenience samples drawn from its database.

Harris Interactive believes that generalizable results can be obtained based on convenience samples by using propensity scoring. As noted in Chapter Three, propensity scoring was invented to deal with selection bias, but has not traditionally been used in the context of surveys. The claim that propensity scoring can successfully adjust for selection bias in volunteer panel surveys is controversial among researchers (see Couper, 2000). Harris Interactive insiders claim to have success with propensity scoring by pointing to accurate predictions of election outcomes (Taylor, 2000).

Berrens et al. (2001) compared an RDD survey with identical surveys conducted by Harris Interactive and Knowledge Networks. Despite the large sample sizes, Berrens et al. found that when demographic variables (including income) are adjusted for via regression, all three surveys yielded statistically indistinguishable results on several questions. On the other hand, in a matched comparison study of results from a conventional RDD survey, a Knowledge Networks survey, and a Harris Interactive survey, Chang (2001) found significantly different results among the three methods. In Chapter Six, we present a case study on a Harris Interactive survey.

PROBABILITY SAMPLING APPROACHES

If a probability sample is desired, how to go about obtaining a sample frame that covers most or all of the target population becomes a crucial issue. The nature of the target population is relevant to our discussion here. We distinguish between closed target populations and open, or general target, populations.

Sampling from a Closed Population

We refer to target populations within organizations that maintain some sort of list of their membership as *closed populations* (for example, lists of company employees, university staff members, or magazine subscribers). It is usually fairly easy to construct sample frames for these groups. Even if an organization does not maintain a directory of its members' e-mail addresses (as in the case of the U. S. Air Force, which is discussed in Chapter Six), there may still be a systematic way of constructing those addresses (for example, firstname.lastname@airforcebase.mil). Or, it might be possible to reach individuals via regular internal company mail. In short, there is usually an obvious way to construct a sample frame, which then makes it feasible to draw a probability sample.

Sampling from General Populations

In this report, we refer to populations other than closed populations as "general populations" (for example, residents of California or patients who have reported adverse drug reactions). Members of general populations are more difficult to contact because a list of e-mail addresses with a wide enough coverage to serve as the sample frame is not usually available. In addition, for the Internet, non–list-based sampling alternatives are not available.[3]

Although e-mail lists with wide coverage are not currently available, that situation may change in the future. Right now, the only way to recruit a probability sample is by contacting potential respondents through some conventional means (generally, by mail or phone). The respondents can then be asked to respond to a survey via the Web (or by another mode or set of modes). The problem with this option is that the cost savings that can be realized through an entirely Internet-based survey process are greatly reduced.

If an Internet-based response mode is used, potential respondents must first be contacted through a conventional mode and either di-

---

[3]List-based sampling approaches require enumeration of an entire population (such as by e-mail address). There are non–list-based alternatives, however. For example, RDD does not require an enumeration of the population, and there are other less-popular methods (for example, area sampling). However, no equivalent to RDD or another similar method exists with the Internet. If such an alternative could be developed, it would mean sending large numbers of unsolicited e-mails. This approach, however, would likely face resistance from Internet service providers and from those advocating against "spam" (junk e-mail), and there would be legal challenges in some U.S. states. In fact, the unsolicited mass distribution of spam *may* be illegal. (Note that RDD is unsolicited phone calling, which is *not* illegal). According to U.S. Code Title 47, Section 227(a)(2)(B), a computer/modem/printer meets the definition of a telephone fax machine and according to Section 227(b)(1)(C), it is unlawful to send any unsolicited advertisements to such equipment. In addition, according to Section 227(b)(3)(C), a violation of this law is punishable by action to recover actual monetary loss, or $500, whichever is greater, for each violation. Whether a computer meets the definition of a fax machine and whether this portion of the U.S. Code actually applies to e-mail spam are controversial matters and apparently have not been tested in court. However, even if spam is legal, there is significant resistance to it within the Internet community to the extent that, once identified, are often denied service by Internet service providers.

If an Internet-based response mode is used, potential respondents must first be contacted through a conventional mode and either directed to a Web site or their e-mail address must be collected for subsequent distribution of an e-mail survey instrument. Given the as-yet-incomplete penetration of the Internet to the general population, this approach currently implies that (1) mixed modes must be used for response so that potential respondents without Internet access can respond; *or* (2) those without Internet access must be provided with the requisite hardware and software as part of the survey effort;[4] *or* (3) researchers must be willing to accept a considerable discrepancy between the sample frame and the target population. Chapter Six contains a case study of a survey in which a general population was contacted via postal mail and then asked to respond via the Web.

Prerecruited Panel

A *prerecruited panel* is a group of potential survey respondents, recruited by some probabilistic method, who are available for repeated surveying. A good example of a firm that uses prerecruited panels is Knowledge Networks, which recruits a panel of individuals via RDD to participate in ongoing surveys. Panelists receive three or four surveys a month requiring between 10 and 15 minutes each to complete. Sampling is controlled such that panelists are not given more than one survey on a given topic in a three-month period.

With both volunteer and recruited panels, one concern that researchers have is that participants may tire of filling out surveys, a condition called "panel fatigue," or learn to provide the easiest responses, a phenomenon called "panel conditioning." There is evidence to support that panel conditioning does happen: Comparing a Web survey conducted by Knowledge Networks and an RDD survey, each using identical questionnaires, Berrens et al. (2001) reported that panel participants gave a considerably higher percentage of "don't know" responses than panelists in the RDD survey. An alternative explanation for the higher rate of "don't know" responses on the Web could be due to the survey mode and design of the

---

[4]For cost reasons, this approach makes sense only for a panel in which respondents can be used again for other surveys.

instruments rather than panel conditioning. Whereas Web surveys typically offer an explicit "don't know," in telephone surveys, "don't know" responses are usually not offered and are often probed when used by the respondent.

A HYBRID SAMPLING APPROACH: COMBINING A CONVENIENCE SAMPLE WITH A PROBABILITY SAMPLE

Because it can be relatively inexpensive to obtain a convenience sample from the Web, it is reasonable to ask whether there are advantages to combining a large convenience sample with a probability sample. The hope is that the resulting larger combined sample might be more precise than the random sample, or that the probability sample can be used to correct any bias in the convenience sample, again resulting in a larger sample and a more precise result. We have investigated this possibility and the details are given in Appendix C.

We found that it is futile to attempt to adjust the convenience sample because it provides no additional information for any subsequent estimation. It is also not useful to combine an unadjusted convenience sample with a probability sample unless the bias from the convenience sample is known to be very small and the probability sample has at least several thousand respondents. Furthermore, in most, if not all, circumstances, there is no way of knowing the magnitude of the bias in advance. Thus, the addition of a convenience sample to a probability sample is not useful in practice.

SUMMARY

This chapter has focused on the most crucial consideration that researchers need to make before conducting a survey: whether they require a convenience sample or a probability sample. Choosing a probability sample has implications in terms of how respondents can be contacted—for instance, advertising on-line or in newspapers is not an option. Except for closed populations with well-defined e-mail address lists or a standardized nomenclature, if the research requires a probability sample, a conventional contact mode (such as RDD) must be used. If a convenience sample will suffice, however, the survey may be conducted entirely electronically.

Chapter Five

GUIDELINES FOR DESIGNING AND IMPLEMENTING INTERNET SURVEYS

Current research on the design and implementation of Internet surveys has yet to produce an authoritative set of rules on constructing and fielding these surveys most effectively.[1] Nevertheless, through trial and error, the state of the art is gradually evolving. We anticipate that over the next few years the practice of designing and implementing Internet-based surveys will be refined significantly.

In this chapter, we provide some guidelines that we have found useful in the design and implementation of Internet surveys. We offer these suggestions as a starting point for making conscious decisions about the specific implementation details of an Internet survey. We base our suggestions on our recent, direct experience with Web and e-mail surveys, what we have gleaned from the literature on Internet-based surveys, and on the general principles of conventional survey practice.

QUESTIONNAIRE DESIGN

The following list provides some tips on how to leverage the plus-points of surveying with electronic media, how to simplify your presentation, and how to design user-friendly input mechanisms.

---

[1]General recommendations for designing and conducting surveys can be found in American Association for Public Opinion Research (1997), Dillman (2000), and Fowler (1993). Chapter 11 of Dillman provides specific recommendations for designing Web and e-mail surveys, many of which we have included in this chapter.

1. **List only a few questions per screen.** Present only one, or very few, questions per screen so that respondents do not have to scroll down to get to the next question. Excessive scrolling can become a burden to respondents and lengthy Web pages can give the impression that the survey is too long to complete, both of which have the potential to negatively impact response rates. However, there is some preliminary evidence that when multiple questions are placed on the same screen, respondents frame their responses to one question in the context of the other questions, and some respondents appear to read ahead before answering the first question on the screen (Fuchs, 2001). This implies that researchers should group questions on a single screen if they desire such behavior or put them on separate screens if they want to discourage it. Also, there is some evidence that using only a single screen or a few screens for short surveys minimizes respondent "abandonment" (starting but not completing a survey) whereas using a single screen and forcing the respondent to scroll down in long surveys increases abandonment.

2. **Eliminate unnecessary questions.** Avoid questions that have answers the computer can determine, such as the date the questionnaire is filled out.

3. **Use graphics sparingly.** In a Web-based survey, graphics can significantly slow the downloading of a Web page, especially if users are likely to connect to the Internet using a modem (as opposed to broadband, DSL (digital subscriber line), or some other high-speed connection). Slow downloads are likely to frustrate some respondents and thereby decrease response rates.[2] For example, Dillman et al. (1998) found that a "plain" survey resulted in a slightly higher response rate than a "fancy" survey. However, as Dillman points out, that response penalty will decrease as overall transmission speeds increase. Alternatively, provide the respondent with the choice of a survey either with or without graphics.

---

[2]This does not apply to the WebTV approach that Knowledge Networks uses because Knowledge Network's surveys are preloaded onto the computer. Therefore, the use of graphics does not slow down the survey process.

4. **Be aware of how respondents may interpret questions in light of accompanying graphics.** Although unnecessary graphics should be avoided, sometimes a picture *is* worth a thousand words. But, when a photo is used, bear in mind that respondents tend to interpret questions in the context of the photo. Care must be taken that the photo does not alter the intended meaning of the question. Figure 5.1 illustrates this point. Respondents may wonder whether the question is asking specifically about grocery shopping or about shopping in general. (Knowledge Networks is aware of this issue and points it out to its clients.)

5. **Use matrix questions[3] sparingly.** With any response mode, matrix questions place an extra burden on the respondent because they require a lot of work to be done within a single screen. Therefore, they should be used with caution. In addition, it is impossible to predict exactly how a matrix question will look on a respondent's Web browser. If displayed poorly, a matrix question may be even more difficult for the respondent to read and comprehend. On the other hand, Couper et al. (2001) found that matrix questions reduced completion time and the number of missing items in the data. Nonetheless, on balance, we feel that matrix questions should be used sparingly.

6. **Reduce response errors by restricting response choices.** Zhang (2000, p. 66) gives examples of how respondents might answer a question about their years of Internet experience (for instance, "3–4, ~5, or 15?"). In this context, Zhang points out that "a predefined response format is helpful to achieve uniformity of data, which will reduce the workload in data cleaning and processing. However, a flexible format may be more respondent-friendly."

---

[3]A *matrix question* consists of several individual multiple choice questions that have the same response options (for example, "Strongly Disagree," "Disagree," "Neutral," "Agree," and "Strongly Agree"). The questions are arranged in a matrix format with each row corresponding to a question and each column to an answer choice. A case study in Chapter Six contains an example of a matrix question.

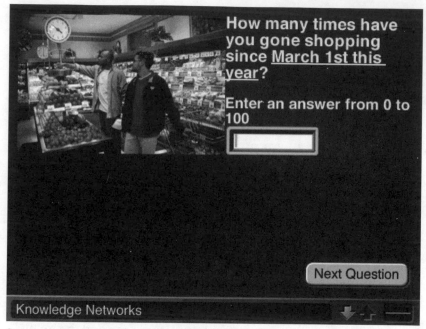

Screen shot courtesy of Knowledge Networks.

Figure 5.1—Use of a Photo to Illustrate a Survey Question

In Web surveys, two tools are used within the Web page interface to restrict respondents' choices: radio buttons[4] (named after the tuner knobs on older radios) and drop boxes. Both are used in multiple-choice questions to which the respondent is allowed to choose only one answer. Radio buttons are useful when the number of choices is relatively small. Because the other choices are automatically deselected when one choice is made, radio buttons reinforce the rule that no more than one answer may be given to a question.

---

[4]*Radio buttons* present several answer choices, only one of which can be selected. If the respondent selects a second choice, the first choice is automatically deselected.

Drop boxes[5] are used when the number of potential choices is large. For example, for the question "In which state do you live?" the drop box could have 51 items.

7. **Force answers only on rare occasions.** With Internet surveys, it is possible to prevent respondents from moving to subsequent questions until they have answered a previous question or completed a previous section. Forcing respondents to answer questions should be used only on rare occasions because the respondent may become annoyed and give an arbitrary or deliberately false answer in order to proceed to the next screen or stop taking the survey altogether. One exception to this rule is for screening questions that must be completed prior to the start of the actual survey. Dillman (1998) also makes this point, although it is one that is often ignored. The advantage to forcing answers is that the researcher does not have to deal with missing data (that is, decreased item nonresponse), but this advantage is more than offset by the increased unit nonresponse. Figure 5.2 illustrates a way to notify respondents that they have failed to answer a question while still allowing them to continue if they wish to do so.

8. **Make error/warning messages as specific as possible.** Ideally, an error message should be placed directly above or below the unanswered or incorrectly answered item. At a minimum, the error message should be specific about where the error occurred and, if possible, the nature of the problem. Redirecting the respondent to a screen that states, for example, "The previous page contains an error," or to a display of cryptic error codes is not desirable. Harris Interactive places an error message directly above the error and even rearranges the items in matrix questions such that the completed items are clearly separated from the missing items.

---

[5]When a user clicks on a drop box arrow, another box with a (potentially large) number of possible answer choices pops up on screen. A user can select his or her choice by highlighting it with the pointer arrow and clicking.

...... You forgot to answer Q2.1 ......

Use the Prev button we've provided if you'd like to answer. If not, click on Next for the next question.

Figure 5.2—Reminder Message to Respondent About a Missed Question

9. **Always password protect Web surveys.** With e-mail, postal mail, and telephone surveys, the survey media provide the means to restrict survey participation that are largely under the control of the surveyor. This is less true of Web surveys because, unless access is restricted in some way, Web sites are open to all browsers and, therefore, the public at large. Thus, user passwords are needed to restrict access and uniquely identify respondents; passwords also can be embedded in a Web site's URL (uniform resource locator, otherwise known as the "Web address") (see, for example, Crawford et al., 2001). Some systems require a user name and password; others require only a password. When only a password is used, it is important to ensure that it cannot be guessed easily.[6] Also, the letter l and the digit 1 are easy to confuse, as are the digit 0 and the letter O (Schleyer and Forrest, 2000). One may want to construct passwords that do not use any of these four symbols or alert respondents to the possible confusion when an incorrect password is entered. Of course, restricting access for a convenience sample does not make sense, so passwords would not be an issue in that case.

10. **Ensure that respondents' privacy and their perception of privacy are protected.** Because there is the risk that transmissions

---

[6]For example, given 500 respondents, a three-digit password is not sufficient. An accidental visitor to the Web site or a mischievous respondent could easily guess a valid password in that case. It is probably best to use at least a four- or five-character password that contains both letters and numbers. There are about 1.68 million distinct passwords, consisting of both digits and letters, that are four characters in length, and about 60 million distinct passwords that are five characters in length, if no distinction is made between uppercase and lowercase letters. Zhang (2000) used a ten-digit password and reports that 91.6 percent of the legitimate attempts by a user to enter his or her password were successful on the first try, and all respondents eventually succeeded in entering a password of this length.

sent over the Internet may be observed by unauthorized users, all survey data should be encrypted. Therefore, after completing a survey, a respondent may be redirected to an "unsecured site" and depending on how the respondent's browser preferences are set, he or she may get a warning about unsecured data transmission. If the respondent is not familiar with messages such as this or does not understand that the survey has already been completed, the respondent may become concerned. A message, such as the following, displayed just before respondents leave a secure area can alleviate any concerns they may have: "Your answers have been securely transferred to our server. As you leave our Web site, your Web browser may warn you about leaving an encrypted site. This is normal. If you get this warning, simply click OK and you will be forwarded to our non-encrypted homepage that you can browse or leave as you wish. If you do not get the warning, do not worry. Your answers will still be securely transferred with no problem."

11. **Provide some indication of survey progress.** With a mail survey, the respondent can easily flip through the pages to see how much of the survey has been completed so far. Without the ability to page through the instrument, or some other means of determining how much of the survey has been done, the survey may appear to have a seemingly endless stream of questions. In this case, a graphical progress indicator (see Figure 5.3) is especially useful.

Crawford et al. (2001) report that progress indicators can have a negative effect if they indicate that respondents are progressing very slowly through the instrument and can add to download time. Further, there is some evidence that for long surveys and surveys in which the indicator is not properly calibrated, the

Figure 5.3—Visual Indicator of a Respondent's
Survey Progress

progress indicators may increase respondent abandonment. In addition, because the meters indicating the survey progress are tied to individual questions, they can be only *approximately* right for any one respondent. (Because of skip patterns, one respondent might answer a different number of questions than another respondent.) On balance, we feel that it is desirable to give an approximate measure of completion at least a few times during the survey. Alternatively, providing a menu that outlines the sections of the survey can also enable the respondent to monitor his or her progress.

12. **Allow respondents to interrupt and then reenter the survey.**[7] Respondents who cannot complete a survey in one sitting should be offered the option of stopping at some point and re-suming later. This allows the respondent to close out of the survey window, go off line, and then go back to the Web site later on to finish. Both Harris Interactive and Knowledge Networks give respondents this option. Some panels do not, including the panels used by the Web survey company Greenfield Online (www.greenfieldonline.com).

13. **Carefully handle respondents who fail a screening test.** Depending on the nature of a survey and the respondent population, access to a Web survey can be restricted until a respondent has passed the screening questions.[8] Unlike with mail surveys, respondents who are ineligible to take a particular Web survey because they did not pass the screening questions may be restricted from even reading the survey, much less completing it. Two possible approaches involve excluding respondents from a survey as soon as they fail a screening question, or allowing all respondents to complete the entire survey and eliminate ineligible respondents later on.

---

[7]This option applies only to surveys with multiple screens. It does not apply to surveys in which the respondent scrolls down from question to question.

[8]If a respondent has a particular interest in completing a survey, there is the danger that the respondent may go back and change his or her answers to the screening questions in order to be allowed to continue. This hazard also exists with mail surveys but not with telephone surveys because respondents cannot change their answers after finding out that they failed the screening test.

14. **Give respondents something in return.** Incentives have been shown to increase response rates. For Internet surveys that do not have an initial mail contact, an incentive might consist of electronic cash or an electronic gift certificate good for purchases from an Internet retailer, or may involve various lottery schemes.[9] The extent to which postal mail survey incentives are transferable to Internet surveys is unknown. For mail surveys, incentives work best when given before the survey is completed, rather than after.[10] Another completely different way of rewarding a respondent is to send survey results via e-mail after the survey is completed.

15. **Take advantage of the media's presentation capabilities.** Options for presenting paper-based surveys are limited by the medium. Generally, they are printed in black-and-white to reduce cost, explanations and special help are minimized to limit the length of a document (or make sure it does not *appear* to be too long), and questions are presented sequentially. Internet-based surveys do not necessarily have these limitations nor do they have to imitate their paper equivalents.[11] For example:

- Hypertext (hyperlinks to other documents) can be used to link "help" screens to detailed definitions or explanations. Thus, via the use of hypertext, additional resources can be made available to the respondent without increasing the apparent length of the survey instrument.

- Color is available at little or no additional cost and, when properly used, can provide visual cues that may simplify the survey

---

[9]A *lottery scheme* implies that only a few, rather than all, respondents receive an incentive. The incentive in lottery schemes is typically much more valuable than incentives that are mailed to all sample members or to all nonrespondents.

[10]In the former case, the incentive appeals to the respondent's good conscience; he or she may feel compelled to respond having already received a reward. In the latter case, the incentive is perceived as a payment for a service rendered. The respondent may then feel that he or she has a morally legitimate choice to render the service in exchange for the payment or not. Because the incentives typically are small, he or she may be less likely to respond.

[11]Note that when respondents can choose to respond to a survey via the Web or through another mode, it is important to keep the two versions of the survey similar in appearance to avoid a "mode effect" from the differing visual layout. Research in this area is ongoing.

process. For example, instructions can be presented in one color, questions can be shown in another color, and help or error messages can be in a third color. But, caution is in order because colors may appear differently when viewed by different browsers, and overuse of color can result in a less-than-professional appearance.

- Certain interactive tasks can be programmed for the Web but are not easily accomplished over the phone or by postal mail. For example, a respondent might be asked to arrange a collection of photos into groups of related photos and then assign names to the groups he or she has created. In another example, the respondent may be asked to peruse a Web site as part of the survey process and then reply to questions about the experience or what he or she may have learned from it. Such responses might enable a researcher to gain insights into how to construct Web sites more effectively.

AUTOMATION

This section offers some tips on employing automation in the survey instrument.

1. **Automate skip patterns.** As with logic checks, make the program (rather than the respondent) manage skip patterns. This will eliminate errors and, from the respondent's point of view, simplify the process of taking the survey.

2. **Automatically validate input, if possible.** *Input validation* is a logical check of a respondent's answers. Logical checks are based on so-called validation rules. Input data validation improves data quality and saves time in data preparation. For example, if the respondent attempts to check both "None of the above" and one of the options in a multiple-choice question, this mistake can be pointed out to the respondent. Or, if the respondent is asked for the year of his or her birth and enters the current year instead, the respondent can be given the opportunity to correct the mistake. However, such validation should be user friendly and simply identify the mistake to the user. As we discuss later, it is important not to force an answer but, rather, if

the respondent chooses not to correct the mistake, the program should accept it and note a data-entry error.

3. **Take advantage of the media's ability to track respondent behavior.** A Web survey computer program can be used to collect more than just respondents' answers. The program can also collect information on how much time a respondent spends on each question or on the whole survey, the number of visits a respondent makes to a Web site in order to complete a survey, the sequence in which a respondent completes survey questions (if nonsequential progression through the survey is allowed), and other such behaviors. This information can be used during pretesting to improve an instrument, and can be used to identify problem areas during fielding and to design better surveys in the future.

4. **Take into account the costs of automation.** Incorporation of logic checking and automatic question skipping may require more-extensive software programs and programming. There are two issues to consider with this: (1) Automated features may be expensive to implement cost-wise, in that they may require a significant amount of programming expertise, and (2) the addition of validation rules means that some respondents' computers may no longer be able to access the survey.

FIELDING

Here, we offer some suggestions on implementing and fielding an Internet survey, including tips on pretesting, problem reporting, and follow-up with respondents.

1. **Thoroughly test the survey.** Because of various, and often unpredictable, software and hardware incompatibilities, it is important to rigorously and extensively pretest any Internet-based survey instrument. This pretesting should include the following:

- Testing using different computing platforms, both Mac and PC, with various hardware configurations.

- Testing with different browsers, including early and later versions of Internet Explorer, Netscape Navigator/Communicator, and the AOL browser.[12]

- Testing with different connection speeds. One respondent's online experience may be very different from another's depending on his or her Internet connection. In particular, the survey should be tested with slow modem connections.

- Testing of skip patterns (particularly when the survey might be filled out in more than one session, test skip patterns in the second session that depend on answers in the first session).

- After the initial responses arrive, double-check to see that no obvious errors were overlooked.

2. **If a large number of respondents are contacted via e-mail, stagger the e-mail invitations.** If numerous e-mail invitations are sent all at once, rather than staggered over a period of time, the Web server will be flooded with responses for the first hour. And if the Web server is unable to handle the onslaught, respondents may be unable to fill out the survey because they won't be able to access the server.

3. **Enable respondents to report problems.** Respondents may encounter unforeseen problems, such as difficulty in accessing a survey with a PIN (personal identification number). Almost certainly, some respondents will experience some type of problem with the survey. Thus, a "help desk" should be established that respondents can contact easily by e-mail and/or a toll-free telephone number. In our experience, the volume of "help" e-mails and phone calls with Internet surveys is higher than what would be expected with mail surveys.

4. **Anticipate potential changes while the survey is in the field.** Changes may become necessary after a Web survey is in the field in two cases:

- When an error in the programming is detected (for example, an incorrect skip pattern or an incorrect input validation rule for the

---

[12]We strongly recommend testing with the AOL browser as numerous problems with early versions of this browser have been reported in the literature.

answer to a question). Changes at this point are undesirable. If the error is not serious, it may be best to simply not correct it.

- When changes to the data the respondent enters are needed (for example, when the PIN that allows access to the survey is loaded incorrectly by the programmer or researcher, or when a respondent accidentally presses the wrong button in the screener, which shuts the respondent out of the survey and does not give the respondent the chance to correct his or her error). In cases such as this, it would be desirable to change the data to allow the respondent to get back into the survey.

5. **Make sure that researchers or survey sponsors can access the Web survey during fielding.** Be prepared for survey sponsors to suddenly decide that they want to take a second look at the survey. Or, researchers may need to gain access to test a complaint from a respondent. One way of ensuring that survey sponsors or researchers can gain access to a survey after it is in the field is to set aside an extra set of passwords just for those individuals.

6. **Remember to follow up on incomplete surveys.** If possible, send a follow-up reminder by e-mail to people who have only partially completed a survey. Respondents who leave a survey halfway through, intending to return to it at a later date, may not automatically appear on the update reports on surveys in progress. At the end of the survey period, data from respondents who did not finish filling out the survey should be retrieved and downloaded to the database.

In the next chapter, we present a number of Internet survey cases, many of which have employed, to a greater or lesser degree, the recommended guidelines we have outlined in this chapter.

Chapter Six

INTERNET SURVEY CASE STUDIES

In this chapter, we present examples of Internet surveys that were fielded by various organizations. Some of these case studies have appeared in the literature and some have not. We present them here to illustrate the range of Internet survey possibilities.

These case studies include probability samples of general populations, probability samples of closed populations,[1] and convenience samples. We included surveys that were constructed using a commercial survey software product,[2] surveys that were programmed from scratch, and surveys that were conducted by a commercial Web survey company.

Although each study represents only one specific implementation of a survey, as a group they all serve to demonstrate the range of Internet survey options that have been tried and continue to be in use.

---

[1]As noted previously in this report, with closed populations it is usually possible to contact survey respondents via e-mail; this is usually not true for general populations because "general" e-mail lists do not exist.

[2]We personally encountered a number of challenges, of a purely technical nature, with a survey software package. Although this experience was limited to a single software package, we believe that the same or similar issues could arise with other such products. The following are a few of the difficulties we encountered: Resizing the browser while the survey is in progress caused the survey to disappear from the screen; after clicking Reload/Refresh, the survey reappeared. It was difficult to make the software display specific error messages in a human-readable format. Displaying explanatory text without an accompanying question was not possible and required a time-consuming work-around. Each response option was preceded by a bullet that could not be removed (this can be seen in Figure 6.3—the bullet is superfluous because each response option also has a check box).

A SURVEY USING A PROBABILITY SAMPLE OF A CLOSED POPULATION

The USAF Surveys Branch, an office of the Air Force Personnel Center at Randolph Air Force Base, San Antonio, Texas, surveys Air Force active-duty personnel and their family members, Air Force civilian employees, Air National Guard and Air Force Reserve personnel and their dependents, and Air Force retirees. The USAF Surveys Branch previously conducted paper-based surveys via postal mail, but it has recently converted to conducting surveys entirely over the Internet. The office is staffed with only four people who are responsible for drafting, fielding, and analyzing surveys of more than 350,000 active-duty Air Force personnel located throughout the world.

The USAF Surveys Branch uses e-mail as the contact mode and the Web as the response mode. E-mail addresses are constructed using a standard Air Force e-mail address format, such as the following: (firstname.lastname@airforcebase.mil. About 70 percent of e-mails constructed in this way actually work, meaning that about 30 percent of the e-mails are returned as undeliverable (for example, the recipient may have chosen his nickname in place of his full first name in the e-mail address or may have added a middle initial). The Surveys Branch also uses e-mail for nonresponse follow-up.

The USAF surveys are administered via the Web. The Surveys Branch developed its own software in SAS (a statistical software package) that automates both instrument development and the generation of HTML code so that the survey instrument can be created easily and then posted on a Web server. Survey responses are subsequently automatically saved in an electronic format that makes it easy to import the data back into SAS for analysis.

Survey topics include personnel, workforce, and quality-of-life issues. The surveys are conducted at the direction of various Air Force organizations and commanders. Survey response rates generally are around 35 to 40 percent—roughly equivalent to the rates the organization achieved with paper-based surveys.

The success of this all-electronic approach is attributable to three factors. First, the standardized e-mail address system provides an easy means to contact a random sample from a closed population that can be completely enumerated. Second, the USAF Surveys Branch has detailed information on its entire population of interest. Third, most of the population has ready access to computers that are fairly standardized, so respondents can reasonably be expected to have access to a Web-access instrument and browser and, therefore, other software problems are minimized.[3]

Under these conditions, all-electronic surveys have the potential to achieve their promise of faster results at lower cost. For example, in response to a congressional inquiry, the Surveys Branch completed an Air Force–wide survey (from initial instrument design through final analysis and reporting) in just 11 days, with its staff of just four full-time personnel. Without the Internet-based survey capabilities, the number of personnel needed to accomplish this task undoubtedly would have needed to be much higher.

AN INEXPENSIVE WEB SURVEY WITH A CONVENIENCE SAMPLE

In 2001, RAND fielded a survey to collect information about victims of sexual assault. The target population consisted of 18- to 35-year-old females who had experienced sexual assault in the past five years. A convenience sample of about 100 respondents was recruited through advertisements in college newspapers and notices posted on support-group Web sites. Respondents were required to call in to receive a password in order to access the Web survey. During that call, respondents were screened for eligibility and, if found eligible, given a password. To protect privacy, minimal information was collected during the initial call and that information and the information collected from the survey were not linked.

---

[3]Interestingly, Charlie Hamilton, the head of the Surveys Branch, told us that after having conducted a number of surveys in this format, the USAF found that two specific occupational groups are difficult to reach electronically: military police and nurses. Neither of these groups, due to their occupational constraints, has easy access to computers with Internet hookups. The USAF Surveys Branch is currently attempting to overcome this problem by oversampling and using additional nonresponse follow-up, but it is not clear whether these efforts can overcome any resulting nonresponse bias.

The survey consisted of approximately 35 Likert-scale[4] questions and participants automatically received an Amazon.com $15 gift certificate upon completing the survey.

We include this case study as a good example of what can and cannot be easily done when fielding a Web survey that is constructed using only HTML and no commercial software. The study topic was clearly a very sensitive one and the target population is one that is generally difficult to identify and reach. The use of the Web and mass advertising was an efficient way to reach a relatively rare scarce population while allowing anonymous survey participation. Programming the ten-minute survey took about three days of a senior programmer's time and about five days of a mid-level programmer's time. Figures 6.1 and 6.2 show sample screens from this survey.

We'd like to start by asking you some basic background information:

Q.1 Please indicate your age:
(please type into the space below)

[   ]

Q.2 What is your marital status?
(please select one)

○ Married
○ Not married but living with a long term partner
○ Never married
○ Separated
○ Divorced
○ Widowed

Figure 6.1—Basic Survey Questions Created Without Commercial Survey Software

---

[4]A *Likert scale* enables respondents to express their level of agreement or disagreement with a particular statement by specifying a value from one to five.

People sometimes look to others for companionship, assistance, or other types of support. Please indicate how often each of the following kinds of support would be available to you if you needed it.

(please select one answer for each question)

	How often would you have...	None of the Time	A Little of the Time	Some of the Time	Most of the Time	All of the Time
1.	Someone to help you if you were confined to bed (had to stay in bed).	● 1	○ 2	○ 3	○ 4	○ 5
2.	Someone to take you to the doctor if you needed it.	○ 1	○ 2	● 3	○ 4	○ 5
3.	Someone who shows you love and affection.	● 1	○ 2	○ 3	○ 4	○ 5
4.	Someone who hugs you.	○ 1	○ 2	● 3	○ 4	○ 5
5.	Someone to get together with for relaxation.	● 1	○ 2	○ 3	○ 4	○ 5

Figure 6.2—Matrix Questions Created Without Commercial Survey Software

The survey is password-protected, and because it was coded using only HTML, the survey instrument is relatively simple. No images are used in the survey, the transmission of data is not encrypted, and error validation is limited (for example, the input of a negative value for "age" will not result in an error or warning message).

If the respondent wished to complete the survey at another time after starting it, her earlier answers were lost. The survey could have been programmed to allow for respondents to temporarily save responses for completion at a later date. In this instance, however, the brevity of the survey did not seem to warrant the additional programming costs this option would have incurred.

The survey featured a button interface that led the respondent to the next screen, but none that allowed the respondent to go back to the previous screen. Upon omission of an item, an error message appeared on a separate screen that read, "Please supply an answer for question *xx*." To return to that question, the respondent needed to click the browser's Back button and then click the browser's Reload/Refresh button to redisplay the previous screen. The respondents were required to submit an answer to every question in order to proceed to the next screen (otherwise a respondent could obtain the incentive gift certificate without answering a single question).

Despite the limitations, this is an example of a simple research survey that was fielded via the Web relatively inexpensively. The researchers required only a convenience sample, and using the Web provided an inexpensive vehicle for anonymous response. Using conventional methods, the researchers would have still recruited participants in the same manner. However, the participants either would have had to be interviewed over the telephone, a much more expensive proposition, or they would have had to provide significantly more identifying information (such as a name and address) so that a paper survey could be mailed to them, which may have deterred participation. Furthermore, use of the Web gave respondents who completed the survey the opportunity to automatically receive an electronic gift certificate, a type of incentive that preserved their anonymity.

Because there is no efficient way to reach this target population, contracting with a Web survey organization, such as Knowledge Networks or Harris Interactive, that can target small cross-sections of the population, would have been a cost-competitive alternative.

A SURVEY WITH A PROBABILITY SAMPLE OF A GENERAL POPULATION AND MULTIPLE RESPONSE MODES

RAND was commissioned in 2000 to study alternative policy options to help improve the military services' ability to recruit enlisted personnel from the college market in addition to the traditional high school market. In response to this commission, Asch (2001) designed a survey that inquired into respondents' desire to enroll in the enlisted ranks of the military under various policy scenarios. The scenarios included various hypothetical incentive packages, such as a monthly stipend while attending college and various levels of starting salaries, and a possible restriction to certain college majors that were desirable from the military point of view and a possible restriction to certain occupations within the military.

Because college dropouts were an important part of the target population, and no obvious strategy exists to reach dropouts, the following strategy was adopted: The sample frame consisted of high school students who graduated or were graduating in 1999 or 2001 and who had also indicated that they intended to attend college. A list from which to draw the sample was commercially available. The sample consisted of 12,500 students graduating in 1999 and 1,750 students graduating in 2001.

With the survey being fielded in early 2001, it was possible to reach current high school students (high school graduation year 2001), current college students (high school graduation year 1999), and college drop-outs (high school graduation year 1999). The disadvantage with this strategy was that all students graduating in 1999 had to be approached via their parents' addresses from two years earlier (or the addresses at which they were living in 1999), which was bound to lead to large nonresponse rates. (Some parents wrote to say that their son or daughter had moved overseas and could not participate or had already joined the military, or to request paper versions of the survey.)

Respondents were initially contacted by U.S. mail and asked to respond on the Web. Only in the second mail follow-up were the respondents also supplied with a paper questionnaire and the option to return the questionnaire by U.S. mail. More details about the follow-ups and the entire survey timeline are given in Table 6.1.

Table 6.1

Example Timeline for Web/Mail Survey

Description	Response Option	Days
Wave 1: Initial letter to 3,000 students	Web only	0
Wave 1: Letter to parents	Web only	7
Wave 2: Initial letter to 11,250 students	Web only	7
Wave 2: Letter to parents	Web only	14
Wave 1: Phone follow-up	Web only	14–28
Waves 1 and 2: First mail follow-up	Web only	21
Waves 1 and 2: Second mail follow-up with paper survey	Mail or Web	36
Waves 1 and 2: Third mail follow-up—reminder postcard	Mail or Web	43–46
Waves 1 and 2: Fourth mail follow-up— replacement survey (including $3 gift certificate to 5,700 students)	Mail or Web	67
End fielding	—	90

Figure 6.3 shows one of the screens from this Web survey. The Web option appeared particularly attractive because the target population consisted of college-bound or college-educated young adults between 17 and 21 years old who were thought to be Internet savvy. Because of the large sample size, this mode was also thought to be cost-effective.

During the time the survey was in the field, several hundred respondents used either e-mail or an 800-number telephone line to contact

2.1 Taking everything into consideration, what do you think you might be doing <u>in the next few years?</u>
(Check All That Apply)

- ☐ Going to college, full-time
- ☐ Going to college, part-time
- ☐ Going to vocational, business, or a trade school
- ☐ Working full-time
- ☐ Working part-time
- ☐ Serving in the active military
- ☐ Serving in the Reserve or National Guard
- ☐ Staying at home or having a family
- ☐ Doing nothing   **6% complete**
- ☐ None of the above

Figure 6.3—Sample Screen from a Recruitment Survey

RAND. Several dozen respondents experienced password problems, however. Most of these problems were caused by the respondents mistaking the letter 'l' for the number '1' and vice versa, or mistaking the letter 'O' for the number '0' and vice versa. Some respondents experienced problems when using older AOL browsers.

The survey setup resulted in a few technical difficulties related to the first-time use of commercial software to construct the Web instrument. In a number of cases, specific features were desired that were not available in the software, necessitating cumbersome work-arounds. For example, the commercial software that was used provides generic error messages. RAND wanted to supply error messages that were customized to the individual question and that would warn the respondent that his or her answer was missing or did not meet a validation rule. The intent was to give the respondent an opportunity to change his or her answer, but not be forced into doing so.[5]

The survey produced 976 eligible responses via the Web and about 1,607 eligible responses by U.S. mail. For the Web survey, an additional 153 responses were found to be ineligible. Adjusting for the fraction of ineligibles, this yields a response rate of about 20.8 percent (62.2 percent of them by postal mail). This response rate should be seen in light of the fact that the majority of the respondents were no longer living at their parents' addresses.

It is noteworthy that there were more responses received by mail than via the Web, even though only the Web option was offered as a response mode in the initial survey mailing. Furthermore, because young adults are thought to be relatively Internet savvy and more likely to respond via the Web than by mail, it would suggest that when respondents are contacted via mail, providing them with a Web response mode is important. For this particular survey, eliminating the mail response clearly would have had a very negative effect on the overall response rate.

---

[5]If the respondent's answer did not fulfill a validation rule and the respondent did not change the answer, the answer was reset to be missing. However, in some situations, the distinction between refusal, missing, and "don't know" may be informative and therefore it is important to distinguish among these categories.

To field this survey on the Web, the following costs over and above the costs for a mail survey were incurred: Programming the Web instrument required eight days of programming work; putting the survey on a Web server and related tasks required another 1.5 days of work; and managing the added amount of interaction with respondents required an additional ten days of survey coordinator time. However, for each survey returned via the Web rather than through the mail, approximately $7 per survey was saved in editing and data entry work.[6] Web responses received in the last couple of days before a follow-up mailing also saved $10 per mailing (including package preparation and postage).

For this survey, the break-even point at which adding a Web survey option was cost neutral occurred at about 580 Web surveys for eligible respondents.[7] This Web survey had 976 eligible responses, and we estimate that roughly $2,000 was saved by using the Web response option.[8] These savings mostly represent the eliminated cost of editing and data entry; only a fraction of the savings is from the eliminated cost for mailings.

A SURVEY BY A COMMERCIAL WEB SURVEY FIRM USING A CONVENIENCE SAMPLE ADJUSTED FOR SELF-SELECTION

As noted earlier in this report, Harris Interactive is an organization specializing in Web-based surveys. Harris Interactive solicits participants via Web advertisements and by other means, and maintains a database of millions of potential survey participants. For any particular survey effort, a sample of Harris's panel is asked to participate. The sample constitutes a convenience sample. Figure 6.4 shows a password screen and Figure 6.5 shows a survey question screen for a Harris Interactive survey.

---

[6]Open-ended questions were not coded on the paper surveys because of cost reasons; if they had been, the savings would have been even higher.

[7]The break-even number heavily depends on the programming time. All else held constant, if the programming work takes five days, the break-even point is at 510 Web surveys; for 15 days of programming work, the break-even point is at 730 Web surveys.

[8]This estimate is associated with considerable uncertainty and should not be taken too literally. This number does not include any fees or revenues on the part of RAND.

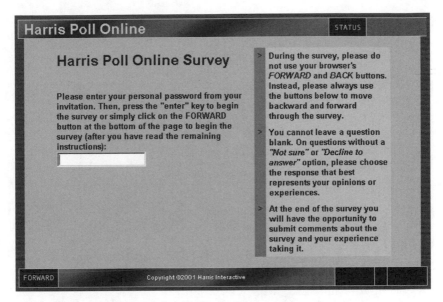

Screen shot courtesy of Harris Interactive.

Figure 6.4—Password Screen in a Harris Interactive Survey

Here, we describe a particular survey that Harris Interactive conducted regarding Californians' attitudes toward health care and health care providers, which was funded by the California Health Care Foundation (Schonlau et al., 2001).

Harris Interactive selected 70,932 e-mail addresses of California residents from its database of people who had volunteered to receive surveys and who had not recently received a Harris survey. A total of 81.5 percent of the selected e-mail addresses were chosen at random from all California residents in the database. The remainder was selected from specific California subpopulations in which oversampling was desired, including subpopulations of various racial and ethnic minorities, those aged 65 years and over, and respondents with low annual incomes (less than $15,000 a year).

The e-mail did not contain the survey but pointed to a password-protected Web page containing the survey. The Web page was accessible only to people with an individual password supplied in an e-mail. The survey was sent in two waves in early 2000 and potential

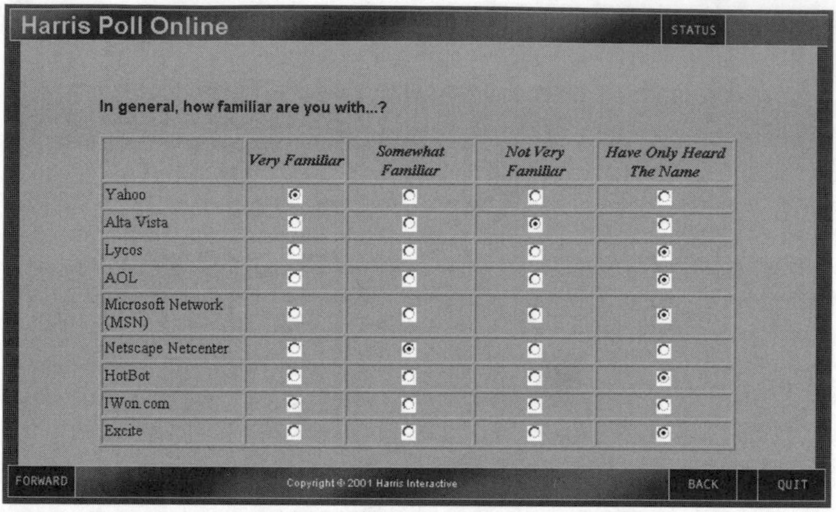

Screen shot courtesy of Harris Interactive.

Figure 6.5—Matrix Question in a Harris Interactive Survey

respondents had almost a month to respond after which the site was shut down. Nonrespondents received one e-mail reminder.

Of the 70,932 persons to whom an e-mail was sent, 2 percent started the survey and did not finish it and 12 percent completed the survey. Only 234 respondents were not eligible either because they were not 18 years or older or they did not reside in California, resulting in 8,195 eligible completes.

Because this type of Web survey does not employ a probability sample, weights are derived exclusively through post-stratification. The stratification matched the Current Population Survey (CPS) for California within race for gender, age, income, and health insurance, and, in addition, for variables derived from the propensity score.

Propensity scoring is a statistical technique (Rosenbaum and Rubin, 1983 and 1984) for comparing two populations. In essence, propensity scoring attempts to make two populations comparable by simultaneously controlling for all variables that are thought to affect the comparison. The Harris Interactive questionnaire included questions that measure general attitudes thought to differ between the on-line and the general population. These attitudinal questions are then used for propensity scoring.

Initially, a Web survey and an RDD reference survey containing the same attitudinal questions are conducted. Propensity scores are obtained by performing a logistic regression on the variables representing attitudinal questions, using an indicator variable (the Web survey or RDD reference survey) as the outcome variable. Respondents for both surveys are sorted into five bins according to the propensity scores. Propensity weights are assigned such that the Web survey's weighted proportion of respondents in each bin matches the reference survey's proportion in each bin. Harris Interactive pioneered using propensity scores as weights (Terhanian et al., 2001). Note that propensity scores can be assigned to any subsequent Web survey that contains the attitudinal questions.

The weighting attempts to adjust for demographic differences of Web respondents compared with the general California population, and also for attitudinal differences of Web users compared with the general population. The key is that, at least in theory, the attitudinal variables compensate for the selection bias resulting from a Web sample consisting of Internet respondents only. The success of this method hinges on several assumptions: (1) the attitudinal variables capture the differences between the Internet population and the general population adequately; (2) no substantial bias is introduced in the event the RDD reference survey (usually targeting the entire U.S. population) is not identical to the target population (which may be a subset of the U.S. population); and (3) no substantial bias is introduced by the fact that the reference RDD typically is conducted a few weeks earlier than the Web survey.

Both Harris Interactive and RAND conducted identical surveys. However, RAND conducted an RDD phone survey whereas Harris conducted a Web survey. We compared several demographic variables for both the RDD and the Web survey with the CPS for California. It turned out that males were overrepresented in the RDD survey (57.5 percent) compared with the CPS (48.9 percent) and Web survey (46.6 percent). Only 9.7 percent of the Harris Interactive sample was Hispanic, compared with 25.1 percent of the CPS and 27.5 percent of the RDD sample. The Harris Interactive survey was conducted in English only, whereas the RDD survey was conducted in both English and Spanish. The Web survey respondents tended to be better educated than Californians overall, based on the CPS.

Weighted-response estimates for nondemographic questions for the RDD and Web survey were different for some questions and similar for others. It was not possible to predict which questions in the two surveys would elicit similar answers. It was clear, however, that questions related to the Internet would yield very different answers. For example, the Web survey estimated that 84 percent of the California population used the Internet daily as opposed to a 24-percent estimate with the RDD survey.

We considered two subpopulations: (1) white respondents who were less than 55 years old, with at least some college, and with an annual income greater than $40,000 and (2) people who use the Internet daily. The estimated attitudes of Californians about health care and health care providers, based on the Web survey and the RDD survey, were closer in agreement for these subpopulations than the estimated attitudes in the general population overall.

We do not consider the RDD estimate to be the "right" estimate. However, it is comforting to obtain the same estimate from two different survey modes. To that extent, we believe the challenge remains to systematically explore the circumstances under which these two modes yield the same estimate.

TWO SURVEYS USING PROBABILITY SAMPLES FROM CLOSED POPULATIONS

The following subsections discuss two case studies of surveys using closed populations.

Prodigy Survey

Werner et al. (1995) conducted a study with an interesting application of e-mail surveys to public opinion tracking. From early 1993 through early 1995, Prodigy[9] conducted 84 e-mail surveys of their customers who were given seven questions about politics and economic issues. Of particular interest, the respondents were asked to "rate the overall job Bill Clinton is doing as president," which Prodigy then compared with the replies to a similar question posed by the Gallup Poll.

Because this survey was conducted with the cooperation of Prodigy, a complete list of e-mail addresses of the subscriber population was available. The survey was sent to a stratified random sample (by age, geographic region, and gender) of Prodigy subscribers with the goal of obtaining 1,200 to 1,500 completed surveys. Unfortunately, Werner et al. do not provide any information about either the initial sample size or the resulting response rates.

The interesting outcome of this experiment is that the approval measure of presidential performance generated by the Prodigy survey and the Gallup Poll survey both tracked in a very similar fashion. This was true even though Prodigy subscribers differ from the U.S. population in that they are more likely to be male, Republican, and married; they are older than the U.S. population on average; and a higher percentage of Prodigy subscribers are college graduates. Although there was a constant difference between the trends in the two surveys, with the Prodigy poll results consistently five to ten percentage points lower than the Gallup Poll results, the trend-line patterns tracked together in a strikingly similar manner.

The Prodigy poll did attempt to adjust for some population differences by post-stratifying and developing weights in order to match the U.S. demographic distribution by age, gender, geographic region, and political party affiliation. The remaining bias can likely be attributed to differences between the Prodigy population and the general population.

The consistency of the trend pattern between the Prodigy and Gallup Poll results is striking. It is tantalizing to think that the additional differential between the Gallup Poll and an on-line poll could be ap-

---

[9]Prodigy is a commercial provider of on-line electronic services, such as e-mail and Internet browsing. During the time period of this study, Prodigy had about 2 million subscribers of which about 1.6 million were of voting age.

propriately corrected for, perhaps using more-sophisticated methods (such as propensity scoring) to adjust for nonresponse or imputation methods to account for missing data.[10] Furthermore, these efforts could be greatly enhanced if a service such as Prodigy collected additional respondent demographic information as part of the service registration process.

Pew Research Center Survey

Flemming and Sonner (1999) describe a polling effort by the Pew Research Center (an independent opinion research group sponsored by the Pew Charitable Trust) that provides an interesting contrast to the Prodigy experiment. Pew recruited two sets of respondents. The first group was the "volunteer sample." It consisted of visitors to the center's Web page who took a voluntary poll, and who then provided their e-mail addresses and agreed to participate in future Web surveys. The second group was the "selected sample" who were initially contacted as part of a random selection in a nationally representative telephone survey. They agreed to participate in future on-line surveys and provided their e-mail addresses. These samples were then used in two on-line surveys conducted in November 1998 and April 1999. Concurrent with the on-line surveys, Pew also conducted national telephone surveys using identical questions but with different participants, which provided a unique opportunity to compare the results of the on-line polls with results from a conventional RDD telephone survey.

Pew surveyed on a wide variety of topics. As with the Prodigy survey, questions about national issues, election issues, and party and candidate preferences were posed, but unlike the Prodigy experiment, Pew results were cross-sectional only. In addition to the questions posed in the first Pew survey, the second Pew survey also asked about "social advances," "technical progress," and "the reasons for America's success" and respondents' opinions about the future of the country. In all of these categories, the researchers found some similarities between the on-line and telephone results, but more of-

---

[10]In the Prodigy experiment, respondents for which either age or gender were unknown were simply dropped from the sample. This amounted to about 8 percent of the Prodigy population.

ten found differences between the two, even after reweighting to adjust for known demographic characteristics. Most important, the differences were not consistent in any identifiable dimension. Sometimes the on-line results reflected more-conservative thinking and other times more-liberal thinking, and sometimes they reflected a more-pessimistic outlook and other times a more-optimistic one.

Summary of the Two Surveys

Traditionally, random samples from the *entire* target population have been used to ensure that a sample is representative of the target population. The Prodigy sample was randomly sampled from Prodigy subscribers, but if Prodigy subscribers are different from the general population, estimates may be biased. In other words, the sample constitutes a random sample for the population of Prodigy subscribers, but only a convenience sample for the U.S. voting population.

The success of the Prodigy experiment has implications for the potential success of convenience samples in general. However, whereas the Prodigy experiment seems to offer the promise of being able to adjust for the bias of an on-line poll, the Pew results seem to indicate that the magnitude and direction of such a bias, for any given question, may not *a priori* be identifiable. These questions are also directly relevant to the Harris Interactive approach discussed earlier.

Chapter Seven

CONCLUSIONS

In this chapter, we offer some concluding thoughts on the future of Internet-based surveys, the issues surrounding the use of e-mail and the Web for research surveys, and certain assumptions concerning performance—that is, are Internet surveys faster, better, cheaper, or easier to conduct than surveys that use more-traditional methods? We also explore a few questions that remain unanswered about Internet surveys.

THE FUTURE OF INTERNET-BASED SURVEY METHODS

Internet surveys are here to stay and will become even more commonplace, with Web surveys continuing to dominate over e-mail surveys. Although some experts predict that Web surveys will eventually replace other survey modes altogether, we anticipate that Web surveys will develop into a distinct response mode, with its advantages and disadvantages, which will have to be weighed against more-conventional alternatives.

A major challenge for researchers will be how to distinguish themselves and their surveys from the plethora of commercial and entertainment surveys on the Web. Commercial surveys will proliferate in even greater numbers because the financial and technical entry barriers to the Web are so low. Thus, just as telephone survey response rates have declined because of the flood of telemarketing and commercial surveys, it is likely to become increasingly difficult to achieve superior response rates when using this medium for research.

To date, most Web surveys in the literature have been conducted with convenience samples or within organizations in which a list of individuals in the target population already exists. By comparison, Internet surveys with probability samples can be fielded by using postal mail or the telephone for initial and follow-up contact with respondents, and then using the Web for the actual response.

Currently, there is no equivalent to telephone RDD for e-mail. Even though the fraction of the population having access to e-mail will continue to grow, it is unlikely that anyone will ever be able to construct a e-mail address in the same way a random telephone number is constructed. However, large commercial e-mail lists may yet emerge that are of high-enough quality to be useful in survey research. In any event, Internet surveys are definitely here to stay.

CONSIDERATIONS IN EMPLOYING THE INTERNET FOR RESEARCH SURVEYS

Research on Internet surveys is still in its infancy. Although we expect the research to grow considerably over the next few years, there is currently very little decisive empirical evidence from which to draw definitive conclusions about the optimal design and employment of Internet surveys.

In research surveys, the quality of the survey process is at least as important as the number of surveys fielded. Therefore, traditional survey methods, including the use of probability samples, formal contact, and follow-up methodologies, and the continuing effort to achieve high response rates (for example, through follow-up and incentives) also apply to Web surveys used for research purposes.

The most important question facing any researcher is whether to make an inference about some larger population based on a survey sample. If the answer to that question is yes, then a probability sample is needed; otherwise, a convenience sample may suffice. If the researcher has established that a probability sample is required, he or she must then determine how to contact the surveyed population or how to develop a sample frame. On-line advertising is not an option for generating probability samples.

In closed populations (see Chapter Four), it is often possible to contact potential respondents by e-mail. If so, it may also be possible to conduct the survey entirely over the Internet, in which case it may be conducted in a very timely manner at relatively low cost. Internet-based surveys of closed populations, particularly employee populations, seem to result in higher response rates than other Internet surveys. This may be because (1) employers are likely to have access to an accurate and complete list of e-mail addresses; (2) completing the survey may be considered part of the respondent's job and thus less of an imposition; and (3) the subject matter may be of direct relevance to the employee or the employee's job, or otherwise considered official business.

For general populations, it is usually impossible to contact potential respondents by e-mail because e-mail lists of the target populations do not exist. This limitation implies that respondents must be initially contacted in a traditional way, such as by U.S. mail, which would then reduce the cost savings and timeliness benefits one achieves with an Internet survey. Furthermore, until the Internet has more-thorough media penetration into the average household, Internet surveys of general populations will typically require a second response mode for sufficient coverage.

Unfortunately, concurrent mixed-mode surveys using both the Web and postal mail tend to result in minimal use of the Web response mode. Further, there is no evidence that this approach increases response rates in any appreciable way (Quigley, 2000). In fact, in two studies we reviewed, the mixed-mode approach marginally decreased the response rates in comparison with the response rates for control groups that only received mail surveys (see, for example, the discussion on the American Community Survey in Griffin et al., 2001).

Therefore, the most effective use of the Web at the moment seems to involve a sequential fielding scheme in which respondents are first encouraged to complete a survey via the Web and then nonrespondents are subsequently sent a paper survey through the mail. This approach has the advantage of maximizing the potential cost savings from using the Internet while maintaining the population coverage and response rates of a mail survey. The drawback is that little is known about the mode effects of Web surveys and the potential difficulties arising from merging data collected via the Web and by mail.

We have argued that for Internet surveys of general populations a second response mode is required to overcome the potential coverage problem. The only exception to this argument is the approach taken by the Web survey firm Knowledge Networks, which has overcome the coverage problem in the United States (see Chapter Three). The only drawback is that Knowledge Networks currently averages response rates of about 25 to 30 percent. Another Web survey firm, Harris Interactive, takes another approach and also claims it is possible to make inferences to general populations, but these claims have not been convincingly demonstrated. It is unclear how the potential problems stemming from low response rates (as with Knowledge Networks) and from using a cleverly weighted convenience sample instead of a probability sample (as with Harris Interactive) trade off. That is, it is not clear whether one approach is preferable to the other.

ADDRESSING CLAIMS ABOUT THE CURRENT PERFORMANCE OF INTERNET SURVEYS

Many assertions have been made about Internet-based surveys that should be qualified. The most common are that Internet surveys can be conducted more quickly, more effectively, and more cheaply than surveys using more-conventional methods. Also, because creating Web pages is a relatively simple process, it is often assumed that Web surveys are easier for researchers to field and easier for respondents to complete. As we discuss in this report and summarize here, these assumptions are not universally true.

Are They Faster?

Web surveys are thought to be much faster than conventional survey modes. This is true when respondents are contacted initially via e-mail, but if respondents are contacted initially through the U.S. mail or by phone there is, at best, only a marginal improvement in overall response times.

When a probability sample is required for a general population, an e-mail sample frame is usually not available. However, once a panel of respondents has been built, such as Knowledge Networks and Harris Interactive have done, Web surveys can, in fact, be conducted very quickly.

Are They Better?

In this report, we discuss difficulties with Web surveys that relate to coverage and response rates and how to overcome them. Here, we point out applications in which Web surveys have advantages over traditional survey modes.

Respondents' answers in interviewer-assisted modes tend to be biased toward socially acceptable answers (de Leeuw, 1992). Web surveys are not interviewer-assisted and therefore, like postal mail surveys, are well suited to surveys with especially sensitive questions (for example, those concerning risky sexual practices).

Subpopulations that represent only a small fraction of a general population (for example, college dropouts) usually cannot be reached efficiently with traditional survey modes. This lack of efficiency translates into high cost. However, the subpopulations of interest may be easily found in the prerecruited panels of commercial Web survey companies. Moreover, because commercial Web survey companies usually charge per completed survey, targeting subpopulations is no more expensive than targeting the same number of respondents in a general population.

If open-ended questions are numerous and important to the survey results, Web surveys are desirable because no coding of the answers is required. There is weak evidence that respondents provide longer open-ended answers to Internet surveys than to traditional surveys. Furthermore, certain interactive tasks can be either programmed for the Web or accomplished in person, but are not easily accomplished over the phone or by postal mail. For example, the respondent may be asked to peruse a Web site as part of the survey and then reply to questions about his or her experiences or what he or she may have learned. The responses may enable the researcher to gain insights into how to construct Web sites more effectively.

Are They Cheaper?

The general notion that Web surveys are much cheaper to conduct than traditional mail surveys is not necessarily true. Web and e-mail surveys can save on some or all mailing costs, but these costs may be a relatively small portion of the overall survey costs. Although Web surveys can serve to eliminate data-entry costs, e-mail surveys may not be able to offer similar costs savings because the survey results often require additional manipulation before they can be downloaded into an analytical database. However, even with Web surveys, the data-entry savings may be partially or completely negated by higher programming costs and the cost of additional help-desk staffing. The literature for the most part neglects labor costs, which can be a substantial cost component of Web surveys. Nonetheless, adding a Web survey to a postal mail survey can prove to be cost efficient.

The marginal cost of adding respondents to a survey is much lower for Web surveys than it is for traditional survey modes. Because of substantial fixed costs, it appears that Web surveys become more economical than mail surveys only when the number of responses reaches a certain threshold. In a mixed-mode setting, in which sample members are contacted by mail and may respond by mail or on the Web, the threshold is probably somewhere between a few hundred and a thousand responses.

If respondents can be contacted via e-mail, the number of respondents required to break even in the cost of adding a Web response option to a mail survey is drastically reduced. (This makes Web surveys particularly appealing when survey panels are used because e-mail addresses can be solicited in the initial panel survey.) The break-even number also declines substantially when a standard Web survey is sufficient, as opposed to one that requires considerable customization. However, we suspect that researchers tend to underestimate the amount of customization that will eventually be needed.

In addition, unanticipated technical problems are likely to arise when a surveyor has no prior experience with Web survey programming and these problems can easily eliminate all potential cost benefits.

Are They Easier to Conduct?

The implementation of a Web survey is much more technically in-volved than that for either a mail or telephone survey. Survey design-ers need to address many issues related to the technical control of Web surveys (for example, how the respondent will move backward and forward among questions, how input validation will be done, what type of passwords will be used, determining which answers are not optional) that are either much simpler matters with conventional survey modes or are not addressed at all. Web surveys also require more-extensive pretesting than mail surveys to ensure that the questions elicit the desired information and the survey program works properly across various browsers and hardware and software configurations. For survey teams without prior experience with Web surveys, conducting a survey via the Web often implies more work rather than less.

SOME UNANSWERED QUESTIONS ABOUT INTERNET SURVEYS

Although the use of Internet-based surveys is growing and will con-tinue to expand, we found that a few key questions remain unan-swered about Internet survey implementation.

What Is the Optimal Instrument Design?

As we noted in this report, little is known about the effects of Web survey instrument design on how survey participants respond to a particular survey question or the survey as a whole, or what sort of design enhances response rates or information accuracy. For exam-ple, at the 2001 American Association of Public Opinion Research conference, some anecdotal evidence was presented that suggested that respondents taking surveys on the Web had relatively short attention spans and tended to browse surveys much as they would browse any other Web site. If true, this would suggest that lengthy surveys or surveys with complex questions may not perform as well on the Web as they would if they were sent by postal mail. Although many of the design principles from paper-based surveys might translate well to Internet surveys, more research is required in this area to confirm this hypothesis.

How Effective Are Incentives?

Although Web survey organizations certainly make extensive use of incentives, there is little mention of incentives in the Web and e-mail survey literature. Web survey incentives can differ greatly from traditional incentives and might include items such as electronic cash or various lottery schemes. With traditional survey modes, it has been shown that incentives are more effective when sent with the questionnaire rather than sent later as a reward for completion of the survey. It is not clear how incentives are best used for Web surveys, or whether they affect nonresponse or measurement error.

How Effective Is Weighting?

The two most prominent commercial Web survey companies, Harris Interactive and Knowledge Networks, both make extensive use of weighting. However, the literature contains little mention of statistical adjustments to reduce various forms of bias. In part, this is because many Web surveys in the literature form a census within a well-defined population (for example, company employees) or because probabilities of selection are equal. Other studies use only a convenience sample and ignore weighting.

Whether a propensity-scoring-adjusted convenience sample is preferable to a probability sample with a low response rate is unclear. There is evidence that convenience samples are effective at capturing relative trends over time.

LITERATURE REVIEW OF RESPONSE RATES

In this appendix, we give a detailed account of the Internet survey literature with respect to response rates in particular. The following sections are structured around the number of response modes that were used in each study (single response mode versus dual-response mode) and by Web versus e-mail response modes.

Single Mode: Web

Studies on the use of the Web as a response mode vary widely in terms of the nature of their target populations, how respondents are recruited, and whether any attempts at statistical adjustment are made in the studies' analyses. In this section, we discuss surveys that primarily or exclusively used the Web as the response mode. We broadly classify these surveys by their method of recruiting respondents: through preselected samples, censuses and probability samples, convenience samples, or hybrid samples. By "preselected," we mean that the respondents were selected and screened to meet specific criteria for responding to a Web survey. By "hybrid," we refer to various or multiple combinations of probability-based and convenience-based methods used to recruit potential respondents.

For Web surveys that used either preselected or probability samples, we compared outcomes in terms of the response rates that were achieved. However, response rates cannot be computed when respondents are recruited through convenience sampling, such as through various forms of advertising, or if the survey is simply posted on the Web for anyone to complete. There are situations in which convenience sampling does allow for the computation of completion rates, which is defined as the ratio of the number of surveys returned to the number of requested surveys. However, in these cases, it is not clear that a high completion rate conveys anything that is particularly meaningful or relevant about the respondents.

We begin by discussing one organization's extensive efforts at evaluating the Web as a survey medium: the United States Census Bureau's Computer Assisted Survey Research Office (CASRO). The U.S. Census Bureau has been actively engaged in research related to electronic surveys (such as CSAQs) for the past decade. The Census Bureau started using CSAQs in 1993 and 1994 by mailing DOS-based diskettes to respondents. From 1996 to the present, CASRO has fielded CSAQs by mailing Windows-based diskettes to respondents and by sending CSAQs via the Web. The first Web CSAQ was conducted in 1997 and, as of this writing, nine more have been fielded, four more are in production, and four are under development. Much of CASRO's completed work, which we concentrate on here, was directed toward business surveys, such as the Industrial Research and Development survey.

Table A.1 lists Web surveys of preselected potential respondents, which are from Sedivi Gaul (2001) and Nichols and Sedivi (1998). With the exception of the Manufacturers' Shipments, Inventories, and Orders Survey, for which the survey team also sent a paper survey in the initial mailing, these surveys were conducted solely via the Web. The table shows that careful preselection can result in high response rates. The exception is the 1998 Company Organization Survey, for which the low response rate was attributed to the use of an encryption level that resulted in many potential respondents not being able to access the survey (168-bit encryption was used versus the more common 128 bit). Lowering the encryption requirement to 128 bit in 1999 resulted in a significantly better response rate.

It is worth noting here that the U.S. Census Bureau put considerable effort into carefully designing and extensively testing these instruments to make them as user friendly as possible. For example, the Industrial Research and Development Survey instrument for the Web was written completely in house in HTML and JavaScript. The program was designed perform real-time branching and editing, opening in its own browser window with "help" information and edit

Table A.1

**Response Rates for U.S. Census Bureau Web-Based Surveys
(Sent to Preselected Organizations)**

Survey	Sample Size	Response Rate
Manufacturers' Shipments, Inventories, and Orders Survey, 2000	73	89%
Company Organization Survey, 1999	194	75%
Company Organization Survey, 1998	48	27%
Industrial Research and Development Survey, 1997	50	68%[a]

[a]After the Web survey phase was completed, paper surveys were mailed to the non-respondents. Thirteen respondents subsequently returned the paper version, for a total response rate of 96 percent.

capabilities built in. Respondents could partially complete the survey, close the application, and then return later to continue the survey. The instrument had a menu bar on the right side of the screen that permitted immediate branching to any section in the survey, so respondents could choose to work through the instrument sequentially or jump around in any order they preferred. In addition to automatically writing the data to a database, the software also recorded how respondents moved through the instrument—information that could be used to improve future survey instruments. Nichols and Sedivi (1998) provide a detailed description of the design and evaluation process.

Table A.2 presents results for other studies that used the Web as the primary or only response mode and used censuses or probability samples. This table shows more-modest response rates than those in Table A.1.

Couper (2001) conducted an experiment in which 7,000 University of Michigan students were randomized to receive a survey about drug and alcohol use; 3,500 potential respondents received a mail survey and 3,500 were notified of an equivalent Web-based survey. Respondents in both groups received an incentive consisting of a $10 gift certificate. The Web-based survey achieved an almost 62-percent response rate compared with a response rate of slightly less than 41 percent for the mail survey.

Table A.2

Response Rates for Web-Based Surveys Using Censuses or Probability Samples

Survey	Sample Size	Response Rate	Population
Couper (2001)	7,000	62%	University of Michigan students
Asch (2001)[a]	14,150	8%	College-bound high school students and college students
Everingham (2001)	1,298	44%	RAND employees
Jones and Pitt (1999)	200	19%	University staff
Dillman et al. (1998)[b]	9,522	41%	Purchasers of computer products
Dillman et al. (1998)[c]	2,466	38%	Purchasers of computer products

[a] Most respondents were contacted via their parents, which reduced the response rate.
[b] A relatively plain Web survey design was used in this experimental arm.
[c] A relatively elaborate Web survey design was used in this experimental arm.

Asch (2001) contacted a random sample of college-bound high school youths and college students by mail (via their parents) and asked them to participate in a Web survey.[1] Nonrespondents were subsequently contacted in a follow-up mailing, which included a mail survey. The study used incentives and several follow-ups, including phone follow-ups to a subset of the sample. The overall response rate was almost 21 percent, of which almost 8 percent answered via the Web. This study is described in more detail in Chapter Six.

Everingham (2001) conducted a "Work/Life Balance Survey" via the Web in early 2000 at RAND. The survey consisted of slightly more than 80 questions about quality-of-life programs. Respondents in two geographically separate offices were initially contacted through an e-mail that contained a link to the survey Web site. Ultimately, 44 percent of the eligible office staff members responded to the survey. Because the target population was employees, Everingham was able

_____

[1] Contacting the sample was complicated and that complication impacted the overall response rate for the survey. In general, the young adults were first contacted through a letter sent to their parents at the parents' last known home address. Parents were then asked to forward the survey material to their sons and daughters.

to compare the demographics of respondents and nonrespondents and the two groups were found to differ only in one dimension: gender. A larger fraction of the respondents was female (59 percent) compared with a fraction of the total population that was female (50 percent) and this difference is reasonably attributable to the survey subject matter. While no equivalent paper-based survey was distributed to allow for direct response-rate comparisons, RAND had previously fielded a paper-based survey on dependent care in 1990 that achieved a significantly higher response rate (more than 90 percent). Whether some or all of the differences in response rates between the two surveys can be attributed to differences in the survey delivery mode cannot be determined.

Jones and Pitt (1999) sampled staff at ten universities whose staff directories were available on the Web. They compared three study arms: contact and response by e-mail; contact by e-mail and response via the Web; and contact and response by mail. The response rates for the three study arms were 34, 19, and 72 percent, respectively.

Dillman et al. (1998) conducted a survey of purchasers of computer products who were at least 18 years of age and had used the Internet from home, school, or work for at least one application other than e-mail in the past month. Dillman et al. obtained a sample of purchasers of computer products and attempted to contact each potential respondent by phone up to five times. Those who agreed to participate were then asked to respond on the Web and were sent an incentive of two dollars. Respondents who initially agreed to participate but then did not were sent follow-up reminders by e-mail (their e-mail addresses were obtained during the initial phone contact). The study had two arms: one using a relatively plain Web survey design and one using a relatively fancy design. (The more-elaborate surveys take longer to load on the computer.) The overall response rates were 41 percent for the plain survey and 36 percent for the fancy one. Dillman concluded that the plain design worked better but also speculated that as Internet access speed increases, this difference may decrease significantly.

There are a number of studies that use convenience samples; often respondents are recruited through advertisements of some form. As we have noted in this report, for studies using convenience samples, response rates cannot be computed or are meaningless. Flemming and Sonner (1999) reported on two Web surveys involving convenience samples. In one, individuals who visited the Pew Research Center Web site were given an opportunity to fill out a Web survey. In the other, respondents to an RDD phone survey were asked if they were interested in participating in an unrelated Web survey. Because both sets of respondents form convenience samples, response rates are not given.

Kaye and Johnson (1999) conducted a Web survey about uses of the Web for obtaining political information. Participants were recruited through newsgroup postings and Web site links. In a social science study of geographic mobility and other related topics, Witte et al. (2000) recruited a large number of respondents: 32,688. The survey design was unusual; it used a base module and four optional extension modules and respondents could elect to answer all of the extension modules.

Vehovar et al. (1999) conducted a large-scale survey targeted at the Internet population of Slovenia, which corresponds to about 13 percent of the country's total population. They sent out 19,000 e-mails and advertised widely in traditional media. Coomber (1997) conducted a survey on the practices of illegal drug dealers. His target population was dealers worldwide. Coomber solicited responses by e-mail and through advertising, and collected responses on the Web (with a very small number of respondents responding by mail) in the hope that the participants would be encouraged to respond honestly because of the perceived anonymity.

Dual Modes: Web and Mail

The number of studies that allow respondents to choose either a Web or postal mail response mode is small. Nevertheless, these studies are important because, for many populations, the fraction of respondents who can answer via the Web may not be sufficiently large to make a Web response option economical, in which case mail is the most-appropriate alternative mode. Table A.3 summarizes these dual-mode studies, reporting the percentage of individuals who responded via the Web compared with the percentage that responded by mail.

Table A.3

Studies Allowing Respondents to Choose a Web or Mail Response Mode

Study	Total Sample Size	Percentage Who Chose to Respond by ...		Overall Response Rate	Population
		Mail	Web		
Sedivi Gaul (2001) and Griffin et al. (2001) (American Community Survey, 2000)	9,596	95%	5%	38%	U.S. households
Sedivi Gaul (2001) and Griffin et al. (2001) (Library Media Center Survey, 1998)	924	95%	5%	38%	Librarians
Sedivi Gaul (2001) and Griffin et al. (2001) (Library Media Center Survey, 1999)	13,440	81%	19%	63%	Librarians
Quigley et al. (2000) (DoD study)	36,293	77%	23%	42%	U.S. military and spouses
Quigley et al. (2000) (DoD study)	36,293	83%	27%	37%	Civilians
Zhang (2000)	201	20%	80%	78%	Researchers
Schleyer and Forrest (2000)	405	16%[a]	84%	74%	Dentists

[a]The response mode in this case was either e-mail or fax.
NOTE: The Quigley et al. entries represent two arms of the same study.

Table A.3 lists the results of two U.S. Census Bureau surveys from Sedivi Gaul (2001) and Griffin et al. (2001)—the American Community Survey and the Library Media Center Survey. In contrast to the respondents to the surveys listed in Table A.1, the respondents to these surveys were not preselected and were also provided with a paper survey. With these surveys, there is a definite negative effect on Web response rates when respondents are not prescreened and when respondents are given another response mode as an alternative to the Web.

The results are mixed for the remaining studies listed in Table A.3. In Zhang (2000) and Schleyer and Forrest (2000), respondents were initially contacted by e-mail; 80 percent of the respondents in the Zhang study and 84 percent of the respondents in the Schleyer and Forrest study responded via the Web. In contrast, the respondents in the two arms of the Quigley et al. (2000) study were contacted via mail; only 23 percent of the respondents in one arm of the study and 28 percent in the other responded via the Web. The studies of Zhang and Schleyer and Forrest typically involve groups of respondents who are largely or entirely computer literate and comfortable with electronic communication. By comparison, the respondents in the Quigley et al. study and American Community Survey study by Sedivi Gaul and Griffin et al. tend to more closely approximate a general cross-section of the U.S. public in terms of computer usage and familiarity.

Quigley et al. (2000) reported on a study by the U.S. Department of Defense (DoD) involving a random sample of 36,293 participants, 52 percent of whom were active-duty personnel, 33 percent were military spouses, 9 percent were civilians working in military settings, and 5 percent were reserve members. The study consisted of three arms, two of which allowed respondents to reply by either mail or the Web. In all cases, the respondents were initially contacted via postal mail. The study design included a prenotification mailing and three follow-up mailings.

In the Quigley et al. mail-with-Web-option study arm, paper surveys were sent out (except with the prenotification) and each contact with respondents (including the prenotification) provided the address for responding via the Web if desired. The final response rate was 42 percent. Of those who responded, 23 percent chose to respond via the Web and 77 percent by mail. In the Web-with-mail-option study arm, respondents were expected to reply via the Web. They were also given the option to request a paper survey, but very few people took advantage of that option. Because of the poor response rate, a mail survey was included with the third follow-up, which significantly boosted the final response rate to 37 percent. Of those respondents, 27 percent chose to respond via the Web and 73 percent chose to respond by mail, and most of that 73 percent responded only to the third follow-up that included the paper survey. In contrast, the mail-only study arm had an overall response rate of 40 percent.

Zhang (2000) conducted a survey of researchers who were scheduled to have their papers published in library science journals. The respondents, who were initially contacted via e-mail, could respond via the Web or could request a mail survey. In the third of three follow-ups, a paper survey was also sent by postal mail. The total sample size was 201 and ultimately a 78 percent response rate was achieved. Of that 78 percent, 80 percent chose to respond via the Web and 20 percent by mail.

The third follow-up generated more mail than e-mail responses, indicating that there is a slice in the target population who will not or cannot fill out a Web survey and will not request a mail survey, but will participate in a mail survey if the questionnaire is sent to them directly. The total number of respondents to the third follow-up was very small (roughly a dozen surveys were obtained by mail and a half-dozen via the Web).

Not surprisingly, a comparison of respondents by response mode showed that those who responded via the Web had a higher self-perceived overall ability to use the Internet, were using the Internet more frequently, and were younger that those who responded by mail. Nevertheless, some of the mail respondents were also highly experienced Internet users.

Schleyer and Forrest (2000) assembled a convenience sample of 450 e-mail addresses in order to conduct a survey about clinical practices among dentists. Schleyer and Forrest obtained the e-mail addresses from large Internet discussion groups for dentists. Their survey consisted of 22 questions that were initially pilot tested. Nonrespondents received three follow-up e-mail contacts. Schleyer and Forrest allowed respondents to return their surveys by the Web, e-mail, or fax; they achieved an overall response rate of 74 percent.

Single Mode: E-mail

In general, the research comparing e-mail with other response modes is limited, most likely because that mode was quickly eclipsed by the Web-based surveys. Most of the e-mail survey studies in the literature are fairly limited in scope and weak in methodology and can be characterized as simple pretests of a new medium rather than careful experimental comparisons of a new survey mode versus existing modes.

However, the literature does contain some fairly rigorous attempts to compare the response rates of surveys delivered via e-mail compared with those delivered via traditional mail. As shown in Table A.4, surveys using e-mail as the sole response mode generally do not achieve response rates equal to those of postal mail surveys.

Note that many of the studies listed in Table A.4 have relatively small sample sizes and that as the e-mail response rate increases so does the mail response rate. This suggests that the improved response rates are likely attributable to an increased overall propensity of the sample to respond because of differences in either the survey methodology or the population. Only two of the studies (Couper et al., 1999; Schaefer and Dillman, 1998) have relatively large sample

Table A.4

Studies Comparing Response Rates for E-Mail and Mail Response Modes

Study	Total Sample Size	Response Rate		Population
		E-Mail Study Arm	Mail Study Arm	
Tse et al. (1995)	400	6%	27%	University staff
Tse (1998)	500	7%	52%	University staff
Schuldt and Totten (1994)	418	19%	57%	MIS and marketing faculty
Kittleson (1995)	153	28%	78%	Health educators
Jones and Pitt (1999)	200	34%	72%	University staff
Mehta and Sivadas (1995)	262	40%	45%	BBS newsgroup users
Couper et al. (1999)	8,000	43%	71%	Federal employees
Schaefer and Dillman (1998)	904	53%[a]	58%	Washington State University faculty
Parker (1992)	140	68%	38%	AT&T employees

[a]Another 5 percent that were returned by mail are not included in this percentage.

sizes, and only one study (Parker, 1992) showed e-mail surveys re-sulting in a higher response rate than mail surveys. However, the Parker study was conducted very early in the course of Internet sur-veying and its results are anomalous.

In a survey of administrative and teaching staff at the Chinese University of Hong Kong, Tse et al. (1995) achieved only a 6-percent response rate with an e-mail survey (with a sample size of 200) but a 27-percent response rate with a survey using university campus mail (with a different sample of 200). In a follow-up experiment, Tse (1998) randomly assigned 500 potential respondents selected from the Chinese University telephone directory to receive either an e-mail survey or an equivalent paper survey sent through the campus mail. The result was a 7-percent response rate for the e-mail survey and a 52-percent response rate for the mail survey. Tse et al. did find an average *initial* response time of about one day for those who re-ceived an e-mail survey compared with an average response time of 2.5 days for those who received a paper survey through the campus mail. The differences in the response times applied only to those who responded to the first survey mailing and not the subsequent follow-up mailing.

The first Tse et al. mailing was followed by a second mailing to all 500 potential respondents, whether or not they had responded to the first mailing. For the mail survey, 64 percent of those who responded via campus mail did so after the first mailing, and the remaining 36 per-cent did so after the second mailing. In contrast, 86 percent of those who responded via e-mail did so after the first mailing and only 14 percent responded after the second mailing. Thus, in this experi-ment, most e-mail survey recipients either responded almost imme-diately (within one day) or they did not respond at all.

Schuldt and Totten (1994), in surveying management information system (MIS) and marketing faculty, achieved only a 19-percent re-sponse rate[2] with e-mail (with a sample size of 218), as compared with a 57-percent mail response rate (with a sample size of 200). Similarly, in a comparison of e-mail versus postal mail surveys,

---

[2]A total of 343 faculty members were in the initial e-mail sample. Of those, 125 were undeliverable. If those 125 undeliverable e-mails are counted as nonrespondents, the actual response rate is only 12 percent.

Kittleson (1995) found that 153 health education professionals, each receiving both a paper survey in the mail and a similar survey via e-mail, were almost three times more likely to respond to the paper survey as they were the e-mail survey (78 percent versus 28 percent).

Mehta and Sivadas (1995) also conducted an experiment involving e-mail and postal mail surveys in which respondents were randomly assigned to one of five groups: (1) those who were sent surveys via regular mail with no prenotification and no reminders; (2) those who were sent surveys via regular mail with prenotification and reminders; (3) those who were sent surveys via e-mail with no prenotification and no reminders; (4) those who were sent surveys via e-mail with prenotification and reminders; and (5) an international group of respondents who were sent surveys via e-mail with prenotification and reminders. Group 2 also received a one-dollar incentive in the survey package.

The most-direct comparison that can be made in the Mehta and Sivadas experiment is between Group 1 (with a sample size of 202) and Group 3 (with a sample size of 60), neither of which received prenotifications or reminders. In those groups, mail surveys achieved a 45-percent response rate and e-mail surveys achieved a 40-percent response rate. A slightly less-direct comparison is between Group 2 and Groups 4 and 5; Group 2 achieved an 83-percent response rate while Groups 4 and 5 achieved 63- and 64-percent response rates, respectively. However, this comparison may not be a fair one because Group 2 also received a one-dollar incentive whereas the e-mail recipients did not.

A number of conclusions can be drawn from the Mehta and Sivadas study. First, e-mail surveys do seem to benefit from advance notification and follow-up in the same way that mail surveys do; in this case, these additional components increased the response rate almost 25 percentage points. Second, because researchers at this point do not know how to most effectively employ incentives for surveys that are conducted exclusively via the Internet, response rates for Internet surveys may continue to lag until the effect of Internet survey incentives is better understood. In any case, employing incentives can prove to be very successful. In this experiment, the inclusion of just a one-dollar bill in the mail surveys increased response rates by 20 percentage points.

In one of the few studies to randomize respondents to response mode, Couper et al. (1999), in a survey of employees in federal statistical agencies, obtained an average response rate of about 43 percent with e-mail compared with almost 71 percent with mail. The experiment conducted by Couper et al. randomized more than 8,000 employees of five different agencies. Couper et al. chose e-mail over the Web as the survey mode because e-mail was almost universally available in the five agencies whereas Web access was often not available. The entire survey effort was carefully administered following TSD principles. In particular, advance notification was provided for all surveys via agencywide e-mail broadcasts and bulletin board notices, mail surveys were followed a week later by a postcard reminder, and e-mail surveys were followed a week later by an e-mail reminder.

Schaefer and Dillman (1998), as reported in Dillman (2000), conducted an experiment involving e-mail versus postal mail surveys of Washington State University faulty (with a survey sample numbering 904). Using a TDM approach, Schaefer and Dillman divided the potential respondents into four groups. The first group was contacted by postal mail only (prenotification, survey, thank-you/reminder, and replacement survey); the second group was contacted by e-mail only; the third and fourth groups were contacted by a combination of postal mail and e-mail. Schaefer and Dillman achieved a 58-percent response rate with the all-postal-mail group. In comparison, they achieved a 53-percent response rate with the all-e-mail group.

Most of the studies we examined conclude that mail achieves a higher response rate than e-mail; Schaefer and Dillman (1998) and Parker (1992) are the only studies we know of in which e-mail achieved equal or higher response rates when compared with postal mail. Parker conducted a survey of 140 former AT&T employees on matters related to corporate policies for expatriation and repatriation. Parker reported a 63-percent response rate with e-mail (63 returned out of 100 sent by e-mail) compared with a 38-percent response rate for postal mail (14 returned out of 40 sent by mail). Interestingly, Parker attributed the difference in response rates to the fact that, at the time, AT&T employees received a lot of corporate paper junk mail but little or no internal junk e-mail. Therefore, recipients of the paper survey were more likely to ignore the survey than were recipients of the e-mail version. With the spread of e-mail spam, the situation is likely to be just the reverse today.

The only other published study that noted exceptional response rates with e-mail is Walsh et al. (1992) in which potential respondents were solicited by e-mail and were offered the option to respond by e-mail or request a paper survey by postal mail. Although Walsh et al. did not conduct an equivalent postal-mail-only survey for comparison, for an e-mail survey of a random sample of scientific computer network subscribers (300 from a total population of 1,100), they achieved a 76-percent overall response rate. Walsh et al. also sent nonrespondents two follow-up reminders and employed a lottery prize of $250 as an incentive.

Walsh et al. found that 58 percent of the random sample replied by e-mail and 18 percent responded by postal mail. They also received requests from an additional 104 subscribers (who were not chosen in the sample of 300) to participate in the survey. Of the self-selected 104 subscribers, 96 percent responded by e-mail. Not surprisingly, Walsh et al. also found a positive correlation between a respondent's propensity to respond electronically and the amount of the respondent's network usage.

Multiple Modes: Web or E-Mail and Telephone

We found no studies that evaluate mixed modes using either the Web and the telephone or e-mail and the telephone. This is not particularly surprising given that Web surveys are often used to reduce survey costs and interviewing by telephone is very expensive. However, telephone contact or response may have other benefits, such as improving response rates, and deserves study in this regard.

SUMMARY OF EVIDENCE IN THE LITERATURE

Detailed information on Internet survey studies that we cite in this report is presented in Table B.1.[1] Some of the studies have multiple study arms, each of which is listed in a separate row in the table. Each study arm corresponds to a different experimental setting. For example, one arm of a study might use postal mail exclusively for contacting individuals, while another might use e-mail to invite individuals to participate in a survey that is done on the Web.

We classified the survey samples into census, random (or probability), and convenience samples. Depending on who the target population is, a sample may be classified as either random or convenience. For example, a random sample of participants in an Internet newsgroup for dentists would count as a convenience sample if the population of inference is all dentists in the United States (including those who do not participate in the Internet newsgroup).

Contact modes are classified as mail, phone, e-mail, newsgroup postings, traditional advertising (such as through newspapers or magazines), Web site advertising (such as hyperlinks in prominent Web sites), or Web.

---

[1]Some unpublished studies that we cited are omitted from the table because of limited information.

Table B.1
Evidence Table for Survey Studies Cited in This Report

Year	Primary Author	Survey Topic	Target Population	Sample Size	Type of Sample	Contact Mode	Response Mode	Follow-up Mode	Response Rate (%)
2001	Couper	Drug and alcohol use	University of Michigan students	3,500	Random	Mail	Mail	Mail	41
2001	Couper	Drug and alcohol use	University of Michigan students	3,500	Random	E-mail	Web	E-mail	62
2001	Berrens	Attitudes on the environment	U.S. adults	13,034[a]	Convenience	E-mail	Web	—	N/A
2001	Berrens	Attitudes on the environment	U.S. adults	1,699[a]	Random	Phone	Phone	Phone	45.6
2001	Asch	Enlistment propensity in the military under different scenarios	College students and college-bound students	14,150	Random	Mail	Mail + Web	Mail	20.8
2001	Everingham	Balancing work and personal life	RAND employees	1,298	Census	E-mail	Web	E-Mail	44
2000	Paolo	Curriculum evaluation	Fourth-year medical students	61	Census	E-mail	E-mail	—	24

Table B.1—Continued

Year	Primary Author	Survey Topic	Target Population	Sample Size	Type of Sample	Contact Mode	Response Mode	Follow-up Mode	Response Rate (%)
2000	Paolo	Curriculum evaluation	Fourth-year medical students	83	Census	Mail	Mail	Mail	41
2000	Quigley	N/A	Active-duty personnel, military spouses, civilians, reserve members	7,209	Random	Mail	Mail + Web	Mail	37
2000	Quigley	N/A	Active-duty personnel, military spouses, civilians, reserve members	21,805	Random	Mail	Mail + Web	Mail	42
2000	Quigley	N/A	Active-duty personnel, military spouses, civilians, reserve members	7,279	Random	Mail	Mail	Mail	40
2000	Schleyer	Clinical practice	Dentists	438	Convenience	E-mail	Web + e-mail + fax	E-mail	74.2
2000	Taylor	Political approval	U.S. population	N/A	Convenience	E-mail	Web	—	N/A
2000	Taylor	1998 U.S election for 23 governors and 14 senators	U.S. population	N/A	Convenience	E-mail	Web	—	N/A

Table B.1—Continued

Year	Primary Author	Survey Topic	Target Population	Sample Size	Type of Sample	Contact Mode	Response Mode	Follow-up Mode	Response Rate (%)
2000	Witte	Social science: geographic mobility, community	U.S. adults age 16 and over	32,688	Convenience	Web[b]	Web	—	N/A
1999	Couper	Organizational climate	Employees of five U.S. federal agencies	4,187	Census	Mail	Mail	Mixed	70.7
1999	Couper	Organizational climate	Employees of five U.S. federal agencies	4,066	Census	E-mail	E-mail	Mixed	42.6
1999	Flemming	Election	Anyone visiting the PEW Web site	N/A	Convenience	E-mail	Web	—	N/A
1999	Flemming	Election	Anyone in prior PEW phone interview	N/A	Convenience	E-mail	Web	—	N/A
1999	Jones	Health	Staff at ten universities	200	Random	E-mail	Web	—	19
1999	Jones	Health	Staff at ten universities	100	Random	Mail	Mail	—	72
1999	Jones	Health	Staff at ten universities	200	Random	E-mail	E-mail	—	34
1999	Kaye	Uses of Web for political information	Anyone browsing the Web	N/A	Convenience	Newsgroup postings	Web	—	

Table B.1—Continued

Year	Primary Author	Survey Topic	Target Population	Sample Size	Type of Sample	Contact Mode	Response Mode	Follow-up Mode	Response Rate (%)
1999	Sheehan	Attitudes and behaviors associated with on-line privacy	Individuals with personal e-mail accounts	5,000	Random	E-mail	Mail + e-mail	E-mail	24
1999	Sheehan	Health Web site purpose and funding	Creators of health-related Web sites	834	Random	E-mail	Mail + e-mail	E-mail	47
1999	Sheehan	Attitudes toward on-line privacy	University faculty, staff, and students	580	Random	E-mail	Mail + e-mail	e-mail	47
1999	Shermis	Telecommunications needs of educators	Members of the National Council on Measurement in Education	585	Random	Mail	Mail	—	36
1999	Shermis	Telecommunications needs of educators	Members of the National Council on Measurement in Education	585	Random	E-mail	E-mail	—	30
1999	Vehovar	Electronic commerce	All Internet users in Slovenia	N/A	Convenience	E-mail	Web	—	N/A
1999	Vehovar	Electronic commerce	All Internet users in Slovenia	N/A	Random	Phone	Phone	—	N/A

Table B.1—Continued

Year	Primary Author	Survey Topic	Target Population	Sample Size	Type of Sample	Contact Mode	Response Mode	Follow-up Mode	Response Rate (%)
1999	Zhang	Scholarly paper submissions	Researchers with in-press papers to be published in eight library science journals	201	Census	E-mail	Mail + Web + fax	Mixed	77.6
1998	Dillman	Past Web sites visited, lifestyles, behavior ("plain" Web page design)	Purchasers of computer products	9,522	Random	Phone	Web	E-mail	41.1
1998	Dillman	Past Web sites visited, lifestyles, behavior ("fancy" Web page design)	Purchasers of computer products	2,466	Random	Phone	Web	E-mail	36.3
1998	Nichols	Economic data of large commercial firms	Large commercial U.S. companies	50	Convenience	Mail	Mail + Web	Mixed	94
1998	Nichols	Economic data of large commercial firms	Large commercial U.S. companies	2,552	Census	Mail	Mail	Mixed	84

Table B.1—Continued

Year	Primary Author	Survey Topic	Target Population	Sample Size	Type of Sample	Contact Mode	Response Mode	Follow-up Mode	Response Rate (%)
1998	Schaefer	N/A	Permanent faculty of Washington State University	226	Census	E-mail	Mail + e-mail	E-mail	58
1998	Schaefer	N/A	Permanent faculty of Washington State University	N/A	Census	E-mail	E-mail	E-mail	48
1998	Schaefer	N/A	Permanent faculty of Washington State University	N/A	Census	E-mail	E-mail	Mail	54
1998	Schaefer	N/A	Permanent faculty of Washington State University	226	Census	Mail	Mail	Mail	57.5
1998	Schillewaert	Attitudes toward the Web	Flemish Web users	110 [a]	Convenience	Traditional advertising	Web	—	0.18
1998	Schillewaert	Attitudes toward the Web	Flemish Web users	67 [a]	Convenience	News-group postings	Web	—	1.68
1998	Schillewaert	Attitudes toward the Web	Flemish Web users	51 [a]	Convenience	Web site advertising	Web	—	0.68

Table B.1—Continued

Year	Primary Author	Survey Topic	Target Population	Sample Size	Type of Sample	Contact Mode	Response Mode	Follow-up Mode	Response Rate (%)
1998	Schillewaert	Attitudes toward the Web	Flemish Web users	125[a]	Convenience	E-mail	Web	—	31
1997	Coomber	Drug dealer practices	Drug dealers worldwide	80[a]	Convenience	Mixed	Web	—	N/A
1997	Kittleson	Health educator certification	Health educators	276	Census	E-mail	Fax	E-mail	N/A
1997	Swoboda	Future risks for the planet and mankind	Internet users	8,859	Convenience	E-mail	Web	—	25
1996	Bachman	Total quality management in higher education	Business school deans and chairpersons	244	Random	Mail	Mail	—	65.6
1996	Bachman	Total quality management in higher education	Business school deans and chairpersons	244	Census	E-mail	E-mail	—	52.5
1996	Comley	Early adopters of technology	3,700 names and addresses purchased from Internet magazine in the UK	1,221	Convenience	E-mail	E-mail	E-mail	9

Table B.1—Continued

Year	Primary Author	Survey Topic	Target Population	Sample Size	Type of Sample	Contact Mode	Response Mode	Follow-up Mode	Response Rate (%)
1996	Comley	Early adopters of technology	3,700 names and addresses purchased from Internet magazine in the UK	1,779	Convenience	Mail	Mail	—	18
1995	Kittleson	Trivial questions for health educators	Health educators in a small professional association	153	Census	Mail	Mail	—	76.5
1995	Kittleson	Trivial questions for health educators	Health educators listed in an e-mail directory	153	Census	E-mail	E-mail	—	28.1
1995	Mehta	Internet communication	Active U.S. users of BBS newsgroups	60	Random	E-mail	E-mail	—	40
1995	Mehta	Internet communication	Active U.S. users of BBS newsgroups	202	Random	Mail	E-mail	—	45
1995	Mehta	Internet communication	Active U.S. users of BBS newsgroups	107	Random	Mail	Mail	Mail	83

Table B.1—Continued

Year	Primary Author	Survey Topic	Target Population	Sample Size	Type of Sample	Contact Mode	Response Mode	Follow-up Mode	Response Rate (%)
1995	Mehta	Internet communication	International users of BBS newsgroups	172	Random	E-mail	Mail + e-mail + fax	E-mail	64
1995	Mehta	Internet communication	Active U.S. users of BBS newsgroups	122	Random	E-mail	Mail + e-mail + fax	E-mail	63
1995	Tse	Business ethics	Administrative and teaching staff at Chinese University of Hong Kong with listed e-mail addresses	200	Census	Mail	Mail	Mail	27
1995	Tse	Business ethics	Administrative and teaching staff at Chinese University of Hong Kong with listed e-mail addresses	200	Census	E-mail	E-mail	—	6
1995	Werner	Presidential approval rating	General population in the U.S.	1,200	Random	E-mail	E-mail	—	N/A
1994	Schuldt	Attitudes toward shareware	MIS and marketing faculty in membership directories	200	Census	Mail	Mail	—	19.3

Table B.1—Continued

Year	Primary Author	Survey Topic	Target Population	Sample Size	Type of Sample	Contact Mode	Response Mode	Follow-up Mode	Response Rate (%)
1994	Schuldt	Attitudes toward shareware	MIS and marketing faculty in membership directories	218	Census	E-mail	E-mail	—	56.5
1992	Parker	Expatriation and repatriation	Former AT&T employees	40	Census	E-mail	Mail	—	38
1992	Parker	Expatriation and repatriation	Former AT&T employees	100	Census	E-mail	E-mail	—	68
1992	Walsh	Scientific activities with computer networks	Subscribers to the Ocean Division of SCIENCEnet	300	Random	E-mail	Mail + e-mail	E-mail	76

Table B.1—Continued

Year	Primary Author	Survey Topic	Target Population	Sample Size	Type of Sample	Contact Mode	Response Mode	Follow-up Mode	Response Rate (%)
1992	Walsh	Scientific activities with computer networks	Subscribers to the Ocean Division of SCIENCEnet	104	Convenience	Mixed	Mail + e-mail	—	N/A
1986	Kiesler	Health and personal characteristics	Recently active computer mail users at Carnegie Mellon University	75	Random	E-mail	E-mail	Phone	67
1986	Kiesler	Health and personal characteristics	Recently active computer mail users at Carnegie Mellon University	75	Random	Mail	Mail	Phone	75

[a]Number of responses.
[b]Traditional and Web site advertising.
N/A = Not available.
— = Not applicable.

HOW EFFECTIVE IS USING A CONVENIENCE SAMPLE TO SUPPLEMENT A PROBABILITY SAMPLE?

The appeal of Web-based convenience samples lies in the potentially very low marginal cost per respondent. Attracting respondents to a Web site does not require expensive labor (as phone calling does) or expensive materials (as mailings do). Furthermore, marginal processing costs per respondent are also reduced because the data are already recorded electronically.

But the disadvantage of convenience samples is obvious—potentially large and unmeasured bias. One solution to this problem may be to use a combined probability/convenience sample.

The idea behind this combined-sample concept is that the same survey would be administered to both a traditional probability sample (with or without a Web-based response mode) and a Web-based convenience sample. For example, obtaining a probability sample with 4,000 individuals and a convenience sample with 10,000 individuals might be no more expensive than obtaining a probability sample with 5,000 individuals (assuming that convenience observations are one-tenth the cost of probability observations).

The probability sample will provide a means of measuring the bias present in the convenience sample, parameter by parameter. With an estimate of the amount of bias, one could then combine information from the convenience and probability samples to yield more-precise estimates than would be possible from the probability sample alone. If the convenience sample is very biased, then it will be nearly useless. This implies that the probability portion of the sample would have to be large enough to stand on its own in a worst-case scenario.

If the bias is so large that it renders the convenience sample useless, then there is a moderate loss in precision. (In the example just given, the standard errors would be increased by 10 percent, hypothetically, because only 4,000 observations were available instead of 5,000.) However, if the bias is small, then there is a "precision windfall," allowing subgroup analyses that otherwise would not have been affordable.

USING THE PROBABILITY SAMPLE TO ADJUST THE CONVENIENCE SAMPLE

Assume a probability sample with X_{1i} that are independently and identically distributed (iid) with mean μ, variance $\sigma_1^2, i = 1,...,n_1$. Also assume a convenience sample of X_{2j} that are iid with mean $\mu + \varepsilon$, variance $\sigma_2^2, j = 1,...,n_2$; the X_{1i} and X_{2j} are independent; ε, σ_1^2, and σ_2^2 are known; and μ is the unknown parameter of interest.

One would naturally consider using information in the probability sample to attempt to remove the bias from the convenience sample prior to combining the data from the two samples to estimate μ. That is, one can estimate the bias as $\hat{\varepsilon} = \overline{X}_1 - \overline{X}_2$, where

$$\overline{X}_1 = \frac{1}{n_1}\sum_{i=1}^{n_1}X_{1i} \text{ and } \overline{X}_2 = \frac{1}{n_2}\sum_{j=1}^{n_2}X_{2j},$$

and then use the estimate to adjust each of the convenience sample observations: $X_{2j}^* = X_{2j} - \hat{\varepsilon}$. Having adjusted each of the convenience sample observations, the mean can be estimated as

$$\hat{\mu} = \frac{1}{n_1 + n_2}\left[\sum_{i=1}^{n_1}X_{1i} + \sum_{j=1}^{n_2}X_{2j}^*\right].$$

For this estimator, one could then ask, what is the optimal allocation of the sample between n_1 and n_2 that would minimize the variance of $\hat{\mu}$? The unfortunate reality is that $\mathrm{Var}(\hat{\mu}) = \sigma_1^2 / n_1$. Hence, the variance of the estimator depends *only* on the sample size of the probability sample, which means that the variance is minimized *a priori* by allocating everything to the probability sample. That is, after adjustment, the convenience sample contains no information to contribute to the estimation of the sample mean, so there is no point in allocating resources to collecting the convenience sample, no matter how inexpensive the convenience sample observations are to obtain.

INITIAL BIAS REDUCTION

If attempting to remove the bias from the convenience sample will prove ineffective, then the only alternative is to use the (potentially) biased data in the estimation. However, as we show later in this appendix, and as one might expect, the bias of the convenience sample must be small. One way to respond to this limitation may be to focus on estimating parameters that are less subject to bias, such as within-subject differences or regression coefficients, rather than population estimates of proportions or means. One can also use post-stratification to reduce bias as much as possible. For example, a small set of items can be included in both the convenience and probability samples that are (1) associated with likelihood of participation in the Web-based convenience sample (for example, age, education, computer use, and other such factors) and (2) likely to be associated with the parameters being measured.

To use the post-stratification variables, one should treat the characteristics of the probability sample as the target and model the relative response probabilities of members of the "convenience sample pool" with given values of post-stratification variables. Weights inversely proportional to these estimated relative probabilities are then applied to the convenience sample only. The design effect from this process will reduce the effective sample size (ESS) of the convenience sample, but the low cost of these observations makes compensating for moderate design effects on the convenience sample affordable.

LINEAR COMBINATIONS OF BIASED AND UNBIASED ESTIMATORS OF A POPULATION MEAN

The previous discussion prompts a specific estimation problem: What is the most efficient estimator that is a linear combination of an *unbiased estimator* (the sample mean of the population of interest) and a *biased estimator* (the sample mean of a population that is biased with respect to the population of interest)?

The notation and initial assumptions are as follows: Let n_1 be the number of observations in the unbiased (probability) sample. Let n_2^* be the number of observations in the biased (convenience) sample. Let DEFF be the design effect of post-stratification weights on the convenience sample. Let $n_2 = n_2^*/\text{DEFF}$ be the ESS of the convenience sample. As earlier, assume that X_{1i} are iid with mean μ, variance $\sigma_1^2, i = 1,...,n_1$ and assume that X_{2j} are iid with mean $\mu + \varepsilon$, variance $\sigma_2^2, j = 1,...,n_2$. Also, as earlier, assume that X_{1i} and X_{2j} are independent; ε, σ_1^2, and σ_2^2 are known; and μ is the unknown parameter of interest. Thus, ε is the residual bias after post-stratification.

We are interested in the estimator $\hat{\mu} = \lambda \overline{X}_2 + (1-\lambda)\overline{X}_1$ where

$$\overline{X}_1 = \frac{1}{n_1} \sum_{i=1}^{n_1} X_{1i} \text{ and } \overline{X}_2 = \frac{1}{n_2} \sum_{j=1}^{n_2} X_{2j}.$$

Therefore, the bias and variance of this estimator are:

$$\text{bias}(\hat{\mu}) = \lambda\varepsilon; \text{ var}(\hat{\mu}) = \lambda^2 \sigma_2^2 / n_2 + (1-\lambda)^2 \sigma_1^2 / n_1.$$

As shorthand notation, let $\Sigma_1^2 = \sigma_1^2 / n_1$ and $\Sigma_2^2 = \sigma_2^2 / n_2$. Note that Σ_1^2 is the mean squared error (MSE) of the probability sample and Σ_2^2 is what the MSE of the convenience sample would be if post-stratification had removed all bias. In this notation, $\text{MSE}(\hat{\mu}) = (\Sigma_1^2 + \Sigma_2^2 + \varepsilon^2)\lambda^2 - 2\Sigma_1^2\lambda + \Sigma_1^2$. The value of λ that minimizes $\text{MSE}(\hat{\mu})$ is $\lambda = \Sigma_1^2 / (\Sigma_1^2 + \Sigma_2^2 + \varepsilon^2)$, which means that the preferred estimator is of the following form:

$$\hat{\mu} = \frac{\Sigma_1^2 \bar{X}_2 + \left(\Sigma_2^2 + \varepsilon^2\right)\bar{X}_1}{\Sigma_1^2 + \varepsilon_2^2 + \varepsilon^2}.$$

The intuition for the form just shown is that observations are weighted inversely to the MSE per observation from each sample. Again, as shorthand, let $\Omega = \Sigma_1^2 + \Sigma_2^2 + \varepsilon^2$ so that $\lambda = \Sigma_1^2 / \Omega$ and $1 - \lambda = (\Sigma_2^2 + \varepsilon^2)/\Omega$. Then, one can write $\text{MSE}(\hat{\mu}) = \Sigma_1^2 (\Sigma_2^2 + \varepsilon^2)/(\Sigma_1^2 + \Sigma_2^2 + \varepsilon^2)$.

Note that as $\varepsilon \to 0$,

$$\text{MSE} \to \frac{1}{\left(1/\Sigma_1^2 + 1/\Sigma_2^2\right)},$$

and as $\varepsilon \to \infty$, $\text{MSE} \to \Sigma_1^2$, the MSE of the probability sample.

Also, as $n_2 \to \infty$,

$$\text{MSE} \to \frac{1}{\left(1/\varepsilon^2 + 1/\Sigma_1^2\right)},$$

which is the minimum MSE possible for a given bias.

QUANTIFYING THE CONTRIBUTIONS OF THE CONVENIENCE SAMPLE

Let UESS be the sample size of an unbiased sample mean with the same MSE as the pooled estimator. Then, one can express it as the following:

$$\text{UESS} = \left(\frac{\Omega}{\Omega - \Sigma_1^2}\right) n_1.$$

Let IUESS be the increment to UESS added by the convenience sample. Then, the equivalent probability sample size increment can be expressed as

$$\text{IUESS} = \left(\frac{\Sigma_1^2}{\Omega - \Sigma_1^2} \right) n_1 = \frac{\sigma_1^2}{\Sigma_2^2 + \varepsilon^2}.$$

Next, define the bias in terms of standard deviations of the probability sample $E = \varepsilon / \sigma_1$. Now consider the simplified respondent where $\sigma_1^2 = \sigma_2^2$ so that

$$\text{IUESS} = \frac{1}{1/n_2 + E^2}.$$

As $E \to \infty$, IUESS $\to 0$, and as $n_2 \to \infty$, IUESS $\to 1/E^2 =$ MIUESS, the maximum possible increment to effective sample size. Note the striking ceiling on the IUESS. It means that an uncorrected bias of $1/100$ of a standard error limits the IUESS to 10,000. This is a pretty sobering result—an unbiased sample of 150 is preferable to a sample with 10,000 observations and a standard deviation bias of 0.1.

CONCLUSIONS

We have shown that there is no point in using a probability sample to remove the bias from a convenience sample. Furthermore, the use of an unadjusted convenience sample to supplement a probability sample may be practical only under limited circumstances:

- The probability sample is large (at least 2,000).

- The convenience sample is inexpensive (no more than 20 percent of the cost per observation).

- The convenience sample is large (at least as large as the probability sample).

- The bias after post-stratification is very low (no more than three percentage points).

From a practical point of view, it is also not clear what the source would be for an estimate of the bias parameter.

American Association for Public Opinion Research, "Best Practices for Survey and Public Opinion Research and Survey Practices AAPOR Condemns," May 1997.

Asch, B., personal communications, RAND, Santa Monica, Calif., 2001.

Bachman, E., J. Elfrink, and G. Vazzana, "Tracking the Progress of E-Mail vs. Snail-Mail," *Marketing Research*, Vol. 8, 1996, pp. 31–35.

Berrens, P., A. Bohara, H. Jenkins-Smith, C. Silva, and D. Weimer, "The Advent of Internet Surveys for Political Research: A Comparison of Telephone and Internet Samples," 2001. Available at David Weimer's homepage at www.lafollette.wisc.edu/facStaff/ (last accessed October 24, 2001).

Bradley, N., "Sampling for Internet Surveys: An Examination of Respondent Selection for Internet Research," *Journal of the Market Research Society*, Vol. 41, 1999, pp. 387–395.

Chang, L., "The Representativeness of National Samples: Comparisons of an RDD Telephone Survey with Matched Internet Surveys by Harris Interactive and Knowledge Networks," paper presented at the American Association for Public Opinion Research, Montreal, Que., 2001.

Cochran, W. G., *Sampling Techniques*, 3rd ed., New York: John Wiley & Sons, 1977.

Comley, P., "Internet Surveys: The Use of the Internet as a Data Collection Method," *ESOMAR/EMAC: Research Methodologies for "The New Marketing" Symposium,* ESOMAR Publication Services, Vol. 204, 1996, pp. 335–346.

Coomber, R., "Using the Internet for Survey Research," *Sociological Research Online,* Vol. 2, 1997, pp. 14–23.

Couper, M. P., "The Promises and Perils of Web Surveys," presentation, RAND, Santa Monica, Calif., July 12, 2001.

_____, "Web Surveys, A Review of Issues and Approaches," *Public Opinion Quarterly,* Vol. 64, 2000, pp. 464–494.

Couper, M. P., J. Blair, and T. Triplett, "A Comparison of Mail and E-mail for a Survey of Employees in U.S. Statistical Agencies," *Journal of Official Statistics,* Vol. 15, 1999, pp. 39–56.

Couper, M. P., M. Traugott, and M. Lamias, "Web Survey Design and Administration," *Public Opinion Quarterly,* Vol. 65, No. 2, 2001, pp. 230–253.

Crawford, S., M. P. Couper, and M. Lamias "Web Surveys: Perceptions of Burden," *Social Science Computer Review,* Vol. 19, No. 2, 2001, pp. 146–162.

de Leeuw, E. D., *Data Quality in Mail, Telephone, and Face to Face Surveys,* Ph.D. dissertation, University of Amsterdam, Netherlands, 1992.

Dennis, M., vice president, government and academic relations, Knowledge Networks, personal communication, San Francisco, 2001.

Dillman, D. A., *Mail and Internet Surveys, The Tailored Design Method,* 2nd ed., New York: John Wiley & Sons, 2000.

_____, *Mail and Telephone Surveys, The Total Design Method,* New York: John Wiley & Sons, 1978.

Dillman, D. A., R. D. Tortora, J. Conradt, and D. Bowerk, "Influence of Plain vs. Fancy Design on Response Rates for Web Surveys," unpublished paper presented at the Annual Meeting of the American Statistical Association, Dallas, Tex., 1998.

Everingham, S., personal communication, RAND, Santa Monica, Calif., 2001.

Flemming, G., and M. Sonner, "Can Internet Polling Work? Strategies for Conducting Public Opinion Surveys Online," paper prepared for the annual meeting of the American Association for Public Opinion Research, Montreal, Que., May 13–16, 1999.

Fowler, F. J., Jr., *Survey Research Methods*, 2nd ed., Applied Social Science Research Methods Series, Vol. 1, Newbury Park, Calif.: SAGE Publications, 1993.

Fuchs, M., "Screen Design in a Web Survey," paper presented at the American Association for Public Opinion Research, Montreal, Que., 2001.

Griffin, D. H., D. P. Fischer, and M. T. Morgan, "Testing an Internet Response Option for the American Community Survey," paper presented at the American Association for Public Opinion Research, Montreal, Que., 2001.

Groves, R., *Survey Errors and Survey Costs*, New York: John Wiley & Sons, 1989.

Henry, G. T., *Practical Sampling*, Applied Social Research Methods Series, Vol. 21, Newbury Park, Calif.: SAGE Publications, 1990.

Jones, R., and N. Pitt, "Health Surveys in the Workplace: Comparison of Postal, Email and World Wide Web Methods," *Occupational Medicine*, Vol. 49, 1999, pp. 556–558.

Kaye, B. K., and T. J. Johnson, "Research Methodology: Taming the Cyber Frontier," *Social Science Computer Review*, Vol. 17, 1999, pp. 323–337.

Kiesler, S., and L. S. Sproull, "Response Effects in the Electronic Survey," *Public Opinion Quarterly*, Vol. 50, 1986, pp. 402–413.

Kish, L., *Survey Sampling*, New York: John Wiley and Sons, 1965.

Kittleson, M. J., "An Assessment of the Response Rate via the Postal Service and E-Mail," *Health Values*, Vol. 18, 1995, pp. 27–29.

_____, "Determining Effective Follow-up of E-Mail Surveys," *American Journal of Health Behavior*, Vol. 21, 1997, pp. 193–196.

Larson, B., "New Jersey Primary Poll," *New York Times*, May 16, 2001, p. A30.

Mehta, R., and E. Sivadas "Comparing Response Rates and Response Content in Mail versus Electronic Mail Surveys," *Journal of the Market Research Society*, Vol. 37, 1995, pp. 429–439.

Nichols, E., and B. Sedivi, "Economic Data Collection via the Web: A Census Bureau Case Study," proceedings of the Section on Survey Research Methods, American Statistical Association, Alexandria, Va., 1998, pp. 366–371.

Paolo, A. M., G. A. Bonaminio, C. Gibson, T. Partridge, and K. Kallail, "Response Rate Comparisons of E-mail and Mail Distributed Student Evaluations," *Teaching and Learning in Medicine*, Vol. 12, 2000, pp. 81–84.

Parker, L., "Collecting Data the E-Mail Way," *Training and Development*, July 1992, pp. 52–54.

Quigley, B., R. A. Riemer, D. E. Cruzen, and S. Rosen, "Internet Versus Paper Survey Administration: Preliminary Finding on Response Rates," 42nd Annual Conference of the International Military Testing Association, Edinburgh, Scotland, 2000.

Rosenbaum, P. R., and D. B. Rubin, "The Central Role of the Propensity Score in Observational Studies for Causal Effects," *Biometrika*, Vol. 70, 1983, pp. 41–55.

_____, "Reducing Bias in Observational Studies Using Subclassification on the Propensity Score," *Journal of the American Statistical Association*, Vol. 79, 1984, pp. 516–524.

Schaefer, D. R., and D. A. Dillman, "Development of a Standard E-mail Methodology: Results of an Experiment," *Public Opinion Quarterly*, Vol. 62, 1998, pp. 378–397.

Schillewaert, N., F. Langerak, and T. Duhamel, "Non-probability Sampling for WWW Surveys: A Comparison of Methods," *Journal of the Market Research Society*, Vol. 40, 1998, pp. 307–322.

Schleyer, T.K.L., and J. L. Forrest, "Methods for the Design and Administration Web-Based Surveys," *Journal of the American Medical Informatics Association,* Vol. 7, 2000, pp. 416–425.

Schonlau, M., K. Zapert, L. Simon-Payne, K. Sanstad, M. Spranca, H. Kan, J. Adams, and S. Berry, "Comparing Random Digit Dial Surveys with Internet Surveys: The Case of Health Care Consumers in California," unpublished manuscript, 2001.

Schuldt, B. A., and J. W. Totten, "Electronic Mail vs. Mail Survey Response Rates," *Marketing Research,* Vol. 6, 1994, pp. 36–44.

Sedivi Gaul, B., "Web Computerized Self-Administered Questionnaires (CSAQ)," presentation to the 2001 Federal CASIC Workshops, U.S. Census Bureau, Computer Assisted Survey Research Office, Washington, D.C., 2001.

Sheehan, K. B., and S. J. McMillan, "Response Variation in E-Mail Surveys: An Exploration," *Journal of Advertising Research,* July/August 1999, pp. 45–54.

Shermis, M. D., and D. Lombard, "A Comparison of Survey Data Collected by Regular Mail and Electronic Mail Questionnaires," *Journal of Business and Psychology,* Vol. 14, 1999, pp. 341–354.

Swoboda, W. J., N. Muhlberger, R. Weitkunat, and S. Schneeweib, "Internet Surveys by Direct Mailing," *Social Science Computer Review,* Vol. 15, 1997, pp. 242–255.

Taylor, H., "Does Internet Research 'Work'? Comparing On-line Survey Results with Telephone Surveys," *Journal of the Market Research Society,* Vol. 42, 2000, pp. 51–63.

Terhanian, G., R. Smith, J. Bremer, and R. K. Thomas, "Exploiting Analytical Advances: Minimizing the Biases Associated with Internet-Based Surveys of Non-Random Samples," *ARF/ESOMAR: Worldwide Online Measurement,* ESOMAR Publication Services, Vol. 248, 2001, pp. 247–272.

Tse, A.C.B., "Comparing the Response Rate, Response Speed and Response Quality of Two Methods of Sending Questionnaires: E-mail Versus Mail," *Journal of the Market Research Society,* Vol. 40, 1998, pp. 353–361.

Tse, A.C.B., K. C. Tse, C. H. Yin, C. B. Ting, K. W. Yi, K. P. Yee, and W. C. Hong, "Comparing Two Methods of Sending Out Question-naires: E-mail Versus Mail," *Journal of the Market Research Society,* Vol. 37, 1995, pp. 441–446.

Vehovar, V., K. Lozar Manfreda, and Z. Batagelj, "Web Surveys: Can the Weighing Solve the Problem?" proceedings of the Section on Survey Research Methods, American Statistical Association, Alexandria, Va., 1999, pp. 962–967.

Walsh, J. P., S. Kiesler, L. S. Sproull, and B. W. Hesse, "Self-Selected and Randomly Selected Respondents in a Computer Network Survey," *Public Opinion Quarterly,* Vol. 56, 1992, pp. 241–244.

Werner, J., R. Maisel, and K. Robinson, "The Prodigy Experiment in Using E-mail for Tracking Public Opinion," proceedings for the Section on Survey Research Methods, Vol. 2, American Statistical Association, Alexandria, Va., 1995, pp. 981–985.

Witte, J. C., L. M. Amoroso, and P.E.N. Howard, "Research Methodology—Method and Representation in Internet-based Survey Tools," *Social Science Computer Review,* Vol. 18, 2000, pp. 179–195.

Zhang, Y., "Using the Internet for Survey Research: A Case Study," *Journal of the American Society for Information Science,* Vol. 5, 2000, pp. 57–68.